A Century of INDIANA GLASS

Craig S. Schenning

Schiffer Publishing Ltd

4880 Lower Valley Road, Atglen, PA 19310 USA

Dedication

This book is dedicated to my wife, Amanda. In no uncertain terms, if it had not been for her continual support and endless patience, this book would not have happened. Thank you, Mandy. This book is also dedicated to my father-in-law, Jack Ford. While we have not shared the same passion for antique and collectible glassware, it was he who introduced me to my first auction many years ago. Thanks, Jack.

Copyright © 2005 by Craig S. Schenning
Library of Congress Control Number: 2005928792

Designed by John P. Cheek
Cover design by Bruce Waters
Type set in Americana XBd BT/Souvenir Lt BT

ISBN: 0-7643-2303-2
Printed in China
1 2 3 4

Published by Schiffer Publishing Ltd.
4880 Lower Valley Road
Atglen, PA 19310
Phone: (610) 593-1777; Fax: (610) 593-2002
E-mail: Info@schifferbooks.com

For the largest selection of fine reference books on this and related subjects, please visit our web site at
www.schifferbooks.com
We are always looking for people to write books on new and related subjects. If you have an idea for a book please contact us at the above address.

This book may be purchased from the publisher.
Include $3.95 for shipping.
Please try your bookstore first.
You may write for a free catalog.

In Europe, Schiffer books are distributed by
Bushwood Books
6 Marksbury Ave.
Kew Gardens
Surrey TW9 4JF England
Phone: 44 (0) 20 8392-8585;
Fax: 44 (0) 20 8392-9876
E-mail: info@bushwoodbooks.co.uk
Free postage in the U.K., Europe; air mail at cost.

Contents

About This Book and Prices

This book is intended to be both a guide and reference for the identification and valuation of glassware items produced by the Indiana Glass Company in Dunkirk, Indiana. This book is not intended to set prices or market values. All values represented within this book are retail values for glassware in "mint" condition.

Assessed value for an item can be affected by a number of factors including the item condition, the market location, the venue through which the item was sold, and the overall appeal of the design or pattern. While so many factors limit the possibility of creating exact pricing, this book can be a guide as to what one could expect to pay for an item. All values have been established based on internet and regional auction sales, internet retail sales, and personal consultation with collectors and appraisers. In some cases, where no sales information could be found, estimated values have been given. These estimated values were based on sales of items with similar pattern styles and overall availability.

All listed measurements are approximate. Measurements have been taken either from original company catalogs or from the item itself. However, because many of the items in this book were hand pressed, actual sizes vary. In addition, dimensions of the same item were known to change over time, sometimes by as much as half of an inch.

Neither the author nor the publisher are responsible for any outcomes resulting from consulting this reference.

The term "reproduction" has been used when referring to patterns previously manufactured by another company. The term "reissue" has been used when Indiana Glass reused their original pattern molds at a later date.

The term "crystal" has been used to refer to the color of the glass, not to the lead content of the glass. All items listed in this publication were made of non-flint, non-leaded glass.

The text and products pictured in this book are from the collection of the author of this book and/or its publisher. This book is not sponsored, endorsed or otherwise affiliated with any of the companies whose products are represented herein. They include the Indiana Glass Company, Lancaster Glass Corporation, Colony Glass Company, Fostoria Glass Company, Tiara Exclusives, and Lancaster Colony Corporation, among others. All information contained in this publication is derived from the author's independent research. Lancaster Colony Corporation, the parent corporation under which Indiana Glass exists, has neither authorized nor endorsed the information presented in this publication.

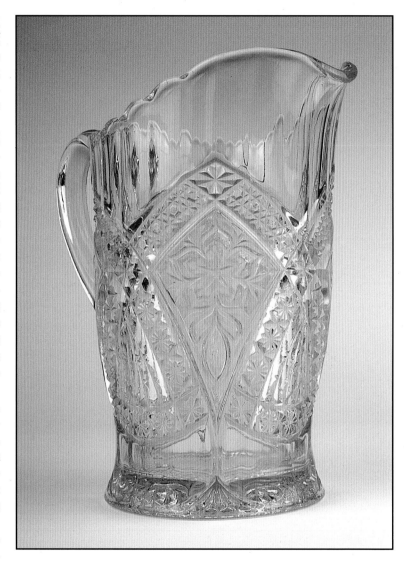

Foreword

The idea of writing this book was conceived through my attempts to find information on glassware patterns that I did not recognize. I realized that there was no single point of information when it came to Indiana Glass products. As I researched and documented information on Indiana Glass, I felt that there might be others needing the same information. So, here it is. I have grown particularly fond of Indiana Glass products since I have undertaken this project. They seem to have been the underdog for many years in the glass production arena. While never quite reaching the "high quality" status of some of the other glass companies such as Heisey, Imperial or Cambridge, they certainly made up for that in the amount of glass they produced over the many years they were in existence. I would venture to say that the Dunkirk facility of Indiana Glass was in continuous operation longer than any other American glass factory.

I stated to my wife one day, "I would bet that there isn't a house in America that doesn't have at least one piece of Indiana Glass." I am sure someone will try to prove me wrong, but the statement gives testament to the quantity of glass that was produced out of the Dunkirk facility. Indiana Glass had the ability to adapt to the ever-changing styles of the time by designing and redesigning molds that appealed to the American consumer.

For the purposes of this book, I have tried to include some basic information with each pattern. That information includes the dates of manufacture, the colors it was manufactured in, the individual pieces that were manufactured, and the approximate retail value of each piece.

Introduction
A History of Indiana Glass

By the time 1896 rolled around, the industrial revolution had essentially ended. The economy was slowing and the threat of an economic depression loomed over the country. However, there were still opportunities for those individuals with enough fortitude and capital to start a new business venture. In central Indiana, opportunities for businesses that used natural gas in their manufacturing processes burgeoned when this new commodity had been discovered in abundance many years earlier. When a large railroad warehouse became available in Dunkirk, Indiana, James Beatty and George Brady wasted no time in purchasing the property. The location was perfect for glassware manufacturing. They had access to seemingly unlimited quantities of natural gas needed for the production process and they had access to railroad lines, which would be needed for the receipt of bulk materials and the shipping of finished products. The Beatty-Brady Glass Company set about the task of manufacturing a variety of clear glass household items.

As the economy continued to slow and the demand for glass tableware declined, mergers and buyouts of glass companies seemed to run rampant. In 1891, the U.S. Glass Company was formed by combining twenty-one glass houses and operating them until 1984. The National Glass Company, which was a conglomerate of nineteen glass factories throughout the Northeast and Midwest, purchased the Beatty and Brady Glass Company in October of 1899 and designated the facility as Factory #1. Under this new ownership, the facility continued to manufacture both commercial and household products. However, trouble lay ahead for National Glass and, by 1907, the National Glass Company had filed for bankruptcy and entered into receivership. By 1908, National Glass had closed its books and the Dunkirk glass facility began operation as the Indiana Glass Company.

While other glass companies were manufacturing carnival glass, Indiana Glass manufactured a variety of patterned glass products and goofus glass. Goofus glass was created by taking clear pieces of pressed glass and "cold painting" the item with various paint colors. These painted surfaces were not treated in any way after drying. As a result, they are prone to a high degree of paint flaking. Finding goofus glass in excellent condition can be a challenge. Businesses at the time used both carnival glass and goofus glass as promotional items, "give-a-ways," or incentives to market their particular product or service. While Indiana Glass appears to have made a few carnival items, it paled in comparison to their production of goofus glass. By 1920, Indiana Glass had established itself as a major competitor in the American glass market, manufacturing numerous household items and novelties, as well as business-oriented items, such as glassware for tearooms, taverns, hospitals, and soda fountain shops. It was this strong footing in each of these markets that would help carry them through the Depression.

Indiana Glass entered the Depression Era with its creation and marketing of the Avocado pattern. Formally known as #601, this pattern began a string of very collectible Depression Era patterns, which included *Sandwich* (#171), *Pyramid* (#610), *Tea Room* (#600), *Horseshoe* (#612), and *Lorain* (#615), among others. All of these patterns were produced in various colors. While the *Sandwich* pattern was a reinterpretation of a classic design, other designs such as *Tea Room* and *Pyramid* were new art deco style patterns appealing to a wide variety of consumers.

The 1930s saw the emergence of the extremely collectible *Hen on a Nest*, or HON as it is referred to in many collecting circles. Always in demand, production of this popular item continued for over seventy years. These hens abound in a seamless array of colors and finishes.

Indiana Glass issued relatively few new patterns during the 1940s. As they had done from the start, Indiana Glass continued to manufacture products for the hotel, hospital, and restaurant industries. Some researchers have speculated that Indiana Glass had several government contracts for the war at that time, making specialty glass products that precluded them from making more consumer oriented products. We do know that Indiana was making a considerable amount of car headlamps. However, with the advent of the sealed beam headlight and Indiana's inability to modify their production equipment to continue in that market, a large portion of the company's income disappeared. After the war, Indiana Glass contracted with Montgomery Ward to market some new patterns for them. These patterns were the 1000 series patterns and they included *MirrorGlas* (#1005), *Lotus Blossom* (#1007), *Willow* (#1008), and *Teardrop* (#1011), among others. However, sales for these patterns were not as high as anticipated and financial difficulties for Indiana Glass began to mount.

The 1950s saw the reemergence of a few older patterns. The *Indiana Custard* (#619) molds were dug out of the archives, the pattern was then produced in milk white glass instead of ivory and reissued as *Orange Blossom*. The *Wild Rose* (#7) pattern was reissued in newer sprayed on colors and Pattern #16 went to the consumer market being called *Weavetex*. As far as new patterns go, Indiana's *Christmas Candy* (#624) pattern was released. However, while Indiana Glass continued making glassware for both home and business, the company was struggling to make ends meet. A lack of financial commitments from contractors, in conjunction with layoffs of both upper and lower level personnel seemed to indicate a gloomy future for the company. However, all of that was about to change.

In 1957, the Lancaster Glass Corporation purchased the Indiana Glass Company, saving it from bankruptcy, and in 1962 Lancaster Glass merged all of its companies into the Lancaster Colony Corporation. As a result of this new ownership a new inventory and sales system was initiated, ending the use of product line numbers and initiating the use of item numbers. It was during this time period that the extremely successful patterns such as *Diamond Point* and *Whitehall* began production.

Indiana Glass entered the 1970s stronger and more successful than ever. Now that Indiana Glass had some room to breath, they decided to try their hand in a new market, the carnival glass market. Since some companies such as Imperial and Fenton were enjoying a resurgence in carnival glass, Indiana cleaned up the Harvest pattern molds and in 1971 began carnival glass production. The molds were used for about ten years, making this pattern in iridescent greens, blues, and golds. The sales were phenomenal. Today, if you search internet auctions you will find an amazing amount of this glassware still available, giving testament to its popularity.

The 1970s also brought about a new sales initiative. In July of 1970, Tiara Exclusives began as a home party plan. Tiara Exclusives was strictly a retail sales organization; they did not manufacture any glass. While Tiara Exclusives purchased its glass from numerous glassmakers, Indiana Glass was by far the largest contributor to this organization. Tiara Exclusives was a wholly owned subsidiary of Lancaster Colony Corporation and was based on home sales to promote its products. Individuals could be "hostesses" and sell the glass products right in their own homes.

The most popular product for Tiara Exclusives was the re-issuance of the old Indiana *Sandwich* pattern. In order to keep abreast of the latest trends in home fashions, Tiara Exclusives sold the *Sandwich* pattern dinnerware in a variety of colors, including red, several greens, peach, crystal, and blue.

In 1979, Indiana Glass purchased numerous molds from the defunct Federal Glass Company. Indiana reproduced Federal's *Recollection* pattern as well as reproducing the *Windsor* line. The *Windsor* products were made in a variety of colors, including pink and blue carnival.

In 1986, Lancaster Colony Corporation made a very significant purchase. They bought the nearly 100-year-old Fostoria Glass Company. Some of the Fostoria molds, as well as several molds purchased from Federal Glass and Imperial Glass, were used by Indiana Glass for the Tiara Exclusives product line. However, the most significant concern for many collectors regarding this purchase was that it now allowed Lancaster Colony Corporation the ability to blend Fostoria's American pattern with Indiana's *Whitehall* pattern. For over seventy years, Fostoria produced their *American* pattern. Over that time Fostoria's *American* became highly collectible. When Indiana first produced their *Whitehall* pattern in the early 1960s, many collectors were upset, but astute collectors could readily tell which company made which items. However, this was a new ballgame. Now Indiana was about to blend Fostoria's *American* pattern with their own *Whitehall* pattern to become the new *American Whitehall*.

Throughout the 1980s and 1990s, Indiana Glass continued to make products for Tiara Exclusives. At the same time, the company was manufacturing and marketing business and promotional style items. Large discount stores such as Wal-Mart and K-mart sold many of their individual glass items such as vases, candy boxes, and candleholders. However, high production costs, worker salaries, and company paid benefits were increasingly becoming an issue for the company and its employees.

In 1998 Lancaster Colony decided to close the nearly thirty-year-old Tiara Exclusives, citing foreign competition and lack of sales as the key contributing factors. Then, in October of 2001, The American Flint Glass Workers Local #501 voted to strike. The strike lasted three months and, while work resumed in January of 2002, it lasted only until November of that same year. Finally, in November 2002, Lancaster Colony stopped all production at the Indiana Glass facility in Dunkirk, Indiana, ending more than 100 years of glassmaking at that location.

The corporate headquarters for Lancaster Colony Corporation is currently located in Columbus, Ohio, and glass products are still marketed under the Indiana Glass name, although most of the products are manufactured at the Colony Glass location in Supulpa, Oklahoma, and Cincinnati, Ohio. The original factory site in Dunkirk, Indiana, is now used primarily for the storage and staging of products marketed throughout the U.S.

Over the years I have met many glass enthusiasts who could not place Indiana Glass in the same category as say Imperial or Cambridge or the myriad other companies that manufactured fine glassware over the years. My opinion is that Indiana Glass constantly recreated itself to appeal to the greater public. Indiana Glass continually walked that fine line between creating a work of art and creating something useful that the average American could afford to purchase and use. The reality is that Indiana Glass did this for over 100 years and the beauty and affordability of their craft will be enjoyed by many future generations.

It is my expectation that the value of glassware produced at the plant in Dunkirk, Indiana, will continue to increase in value as demand increases for items that are no longer produced. It is also my hope that this book will be a valuable resource to those wishing to educate themselves and/or collect the many wonderful products of the Indiana Glass Company.

Shape and Item Definitions

General Shapes

Belled – any round-bottomed item with a flared top.

Cupped - any round-bottomed item, which is smaller at the top than at its widest point. The upper edge is curved slightly inward.

Flared – any round-bottom item where the upper edge spreads outward.

Tapered – any item that is cone-shaped or has a "V" shaped bowl.

Rolled – a treatment affecting the rim of the glass where the edge is turned. This curve may be slight or dramatic, depending on the artisan.

Scalloped – a treatment affecting the rim of the glass where the edge is pinched.

Individual Items

Berry bowl, individual – a small bowl used for serving berries, usually 4 - 5" in diameter.

Berry bowl, master – a large bowl used for serving berries, usually 8 - 10" in diameter.

Bobesche – a glass receptacle at the bottom of a lamp used to collect wax and hang prisms.

Bon Bon – a small candy dish usually less than 7" in diameter. This dish is sometimes called a mint bowl.

Cereal bowl – a medium size bowl used for cereal, usually 5 - 7" in diameter.

Celery – a low oval or oblong bowl typically 8 - 10" in length.

Celery Vase – an upright vessel, sometimes footed, usually handled, and similar to a spooner.

Claret – a stemmed drinking vessel typically used to serve wines and usually holding 6 to 10 oz.

Cocktail – a short, broad tumbler typically used for serving mixed drinks.

Comport – this is usually a high-footed bowl used for serving mixed fruits.

Compote – this is usually a low-footed bowl used for serving mixed fruits.

Cordial – stemmed drinking vessel typically used to serve liquors and usually holding 1 to 1.5 oz.

Cream soup bowl – a medium size bowl with a wide flat lip used for soup, usually 6 - 8" in diameter.

Cruet – a vessel used to pour oil or vinegar. Usually has an associated stopper or cap. In most cases when there are two different size cruets, the smaller cruet was designated for the oil and the larger cruet designated for the vinegar.

Epergne – footed bowl (or compote) with candle cup to hold a small floral vase in the center. The vase may be called a "lily" or "flower" vase insert. A "pegged lily vase," "pegged vase" or simply "peg vase" indicates the base is shaped with an indented form or "peg" so the vase will fit more securely in the candle cup.

Finial – a decorative handle or knob usually found on a lid/cover.

Fruit Tray – a center-handled sandwich tray with the outer edge cupped up.

Goblet – a stemmed drinking vessel typically used to serve water and usually holding 9 to 12 oz.

Jug – a pitcher with straight sides and flat bottom. It may or may not have an ice-lip, meaning a curved-in pouring lip edge to keep ice cubes from falling into the glass.

Lily Bowl – a shallow, somewhat flat bowl with curved (cupped) upper sides/rim. A bowl used for floating flower blossoms.

Luncheon Plate – a plate usually 8" - 9" in diameter.

Nappy – a very shallow bowl or dish, usually handled, used for holding nuts or mints.

Olive – a small bowl in various shapes used for serving olives.

Oyster Cocktail – a low-stemmed or no-stem vessel used to serve oysters or other seafood.

Parfait – a low-stemmed slender vessel used to serve layered desserts.

Pickle – a low oval or oblong bowl typically less than 8" in length.

Rose Bowl – a bowl that is typically shaped like a ball or globe with a smaller than average opening in the top. It was originally designed to hold dried rose petals.

Salad Plate – a plate usually 8" - 9" in diameter.

Salt Dip – a small flat bowl, usually only 1.5" to 2" in diameter, meant for holding salt.

Salver – a high or low-footed flat plate. This item is sometimes referred to as a cake stand.

Sandwich Plate or Tray – a large, flat plate usually measuring more than 11" in diameter. These plates often have two side handles or a center-handle.

Sherbet – a low-stemmed vessel used to serve sherbet or other ice creams and desserts.

Spooner – a vessel, similar to a sugar, used to hold spoons. It may also be a jar with loops around the top edge, through which spoons could be hung.

Torte/Buffet Plate – a large, flat plate, usually low footed and generally measuring more than 12" in diameter.

Tumbler – a drinking vessel, which may be footed with a short stem, footed with no stem, or flat bottomed.

Whiskey – a small tumbler used for serving hard liquor and typically holding 1 to 1.5 ounces. Most people refer to this as a shot glass.

Wine – a stemmed drinking vessel typically used to serve wines and usually holding 3 to 6 oz.

Sets

Berry Set – manufactured prior to the Depression Era, berry sets consisted of a large or master berry bowl, usually 8 - 9" in diameter, and four to eight individual berry bowls, usually 4 - 5" in diameter.

Beverage Set – manufactured primarily from the 1960s on, beverage sets consisted of four to eight ice tea glasses, cocktail glasses, tumblers, goblets or wines. Similar to a water set without the pitcher.

Breakfast Set – manufactured prior to the Depression Era, breakfast sets consisted of a sugar, creamer, spooner, and butter.

Condiment Set – manufactured mainly after the Depression Era, condiment sets consisted of cruets, marmalades, mustards, salt and pepper shakers, and other items on a tray or unit designed to keep the items together.

Console Set – manufactured mostly during the Depression Era, console sets consisted of a large center bowl and a pair of coordinating candleholders.

Luncheon Set – manufactured mostly during the Depression Era, luncheon sets usually sold as a service for four and consisted of salad or luncheon plates, cups, saucers, a sandwich plate, a sugar, and a creamer.

Punch Set – manufactured from the late 1800s to the present, older punch sets consisted of a large 4 to 8 qt. bowl, a 12 - 15" underplate, eight to twelve punch cups, and a ladle. More recent punch sets included a 4 to 8 qt. bowl, eight to twelve punch cups, and a ladle. More recent punch sets usually were not manufactured with a matching underplate. Instead, the punch sets were distributed with hooks to hang the punch cups on the side of the bowl.

Snack Set – manufactured from the 1950s through the 1970s, snack sets consisted of four 8 - 10" plates with a cup indentation and four matching cups.

Water Set – manufactured from the late 1800s to the present, water sets consisted of a pitcher or jug and four to eight goblets or tumblers.

Identifying Indiana Glass

Trying to identify Indiana Glass is not necessarily the easiest task, but I will try to simplify it by providing some general understandings about their products and identify some things to look for when evaluating a potential piece of Indiana Glass.

First, with the exception of the "Tiara Exclusives" mark found on some glassware items, Indiana Glass did not use a permanent mold mark or an impressed mark. The "Tiara Exclusives" mark did not come into use until the late 1980s. However, as mentioned earlier, Tiara Exclusives did not manufacture any glass. They were simply a distributor of glassware products. While Indiana Glass was their primary supplier, a number of other glass companies sold their glass products through Tiara. As a result, I view the "Tiara Exclusives" impressed mark more as a company trademark rather than a manufacturer's mark.

I have on many occasions helped novice collectors understand that the "IG" mark found on many glass pieces is not Indiana Glass, but rather Imperial Glass. Indiana Glass did not use an impressed mark. Beginning in the 1940s, Indiana Glass did use a variety of applied labels to identify their glass, but you just do not find too many pieces with these applied labels. Since the majority of glassware produced by Indiana Glass was utilitarian in nature, the first thing the consumer did after purchasing the glass item was to remove the sticker.

With the absence of a label, there are a few "characteristics" you can look for in order to try to determine whether the item you have found is Indiana Glass. First, you can look at the molding of the item. Indiana did not do a lot of polishing or "cleaning up" of their glass. Many Indiana Glass items have rough mold lines. Only a small percentage of the wares that Indiana produced were polished and/or finished prior to distribution. This practice, or lack thereof, helped keep the price low, thereby making it more affordable to the general public.

A second characteristic to consider is the weight or the thickness of the glass. With the exception of the Depression Era glass, Indiana Glass did not make thin glass items. Their products were heavy and thick and made to withstand many years of use.

One last characteristic to consider is the clarity of the glass. Indiana Glass did not refine their glass to the same degree as some of the other glass houses such as Heisey and Cambridge. Therefore, Indiana Glass products may not have the same brilliance or glass clarity their contemporaries did.

Label for Indiana Glass.

Impressed mark for Tiara Exclusives.

Impressed mark for Imperial Glass.

Label for Indiana Glass.

Label for Tiara Exclusives.

Colors

Over the years, Indiana Glass produced a wide assortment of glassware patterns in a seemingly endless array of colors. Indiana Glass knew that as consumers we are visually oriented and are always looking for something new and exciting. With this in mind, Indiana Glass wanted to make as many of their products appeal to as many consumers as possible.

Making new molds was expensive and not necessarily the most inexpensive way to lure the consumer into the retail store. The less expensive alternative was simply to change the appearance (color) of what they already had. This idea really hit the public's eye with Tiara Exclusives, where Indiana Glass took already existing patterns, made them in a variety of colors, and marketed them with contemporary names.

Many of these colors were produced for just a short period of time. Therefore, in many cases, we can narrow down the time of manufacture based on the color of the item. The colors pictured in this chapter are only a portion of the many colors that Indiana produced.

Indiana also produced many items with colored stains and this is probably a good time to discuss the difference between staining and flashing. In order for glassware manufacturers to provide some variety to the consumer, many glass companies would add colored bands (usually ruby) or would add color to some of the details in the pressed pattern. Glasshouses could do this in one of two ways. Either they could flash the color onto the glass or they could stain the glass. Flashing was a more expensive way of achieving the same goal. In flashing, a thin layer of colored glass is heat applied to the product, which is then polished and finished. Because the color is in the glass, it will not wear. However, you can scratch or chip through this layer of glass to the clear glass underneath. This process required more bulk material, was more labor intensive, and therefore was more expensive to the consumer. Stains on the other hand, were painted on and then the product was reheated to make the stain semi-permanent.

My research has indicated that Indiana Glass only used stains to decorate their glassware. Again, it was Indiana's goal to make their glassware affordable to the average consumer. The unfortunate fault with staining is that it does not last forever. This is easily seen with the earlier pressed glass patterns that had gold staining around the rims. Over the years, just through normal handling, this stain wears. There have only been a few items that I have seen which I would consider to have mint staining. Indiana used blue, green, red, ruby, cranberry, yellow, and gold, as well as a few others. Many patterns such as *Bird and Strawberry*, *King's Crown*, *Diamond Point*, and *Late Paneled Grape* used many of these colors. My research has indicated that Indiana did not flash any of their glassware items.

Amber or Golden Amber, 1926-1931, 1963-1998.

Amethyst, 1975-1986.

Avocado or Olive Green, 1963-1998.

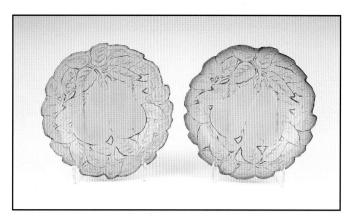

Burnt Honey, 1978-1982.

Bicentennial Blue, 1976.

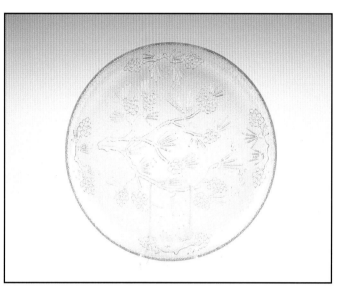

Chantilly Green, 1982-1991.

Black, 1923-1933, 1974-1994.

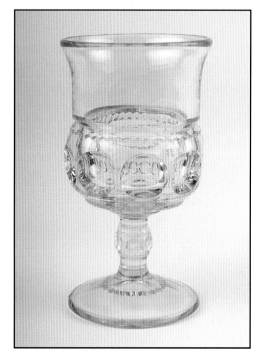

Crystal, 1896-2002.

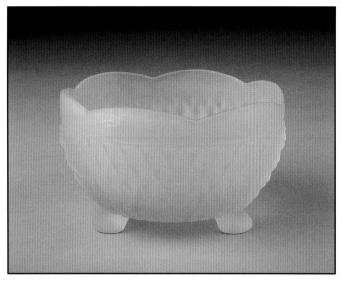

Crystal Etched, 1943-1988.

Fired-On Ruby, 1930s, 1960s-1980s.

Fired-On Blue, 1950s.

Frosty Mint, 1966-1970.

Fired-On Pink, 1950s.

Green, 1923-1939.

Ice Blue, 1982-1987.

Iridescent Amethyst, 1974-1982.

Iridescent Blue, 1974-1982.

Ice Green, 1982-1987.

Iridescent Gold, 1971-1982.

Iridescent Teal, 1980s.

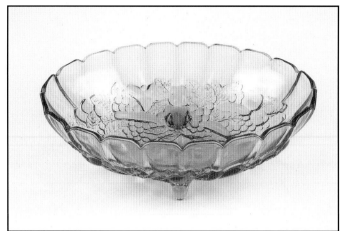

Late Pink, 1990s.

Milk White, 1957-1998.

Light Blue, 1990s.

Pewtertone, 1966-1970.

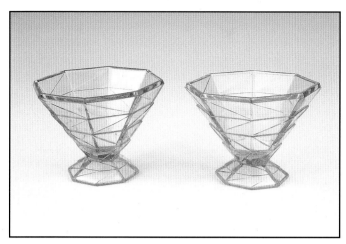

Pink, 1923-1933.

Sunset, 1974-1982.

Spruce Green, 1989-1998.

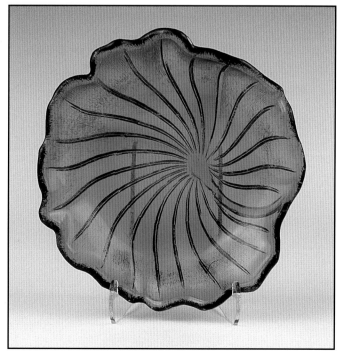

Teal, 1980s.

Terrace Green, 1950s.

Yellow, 1929-1939.

Wildfire, late 1970s-early 1980s.

Yellow Mist, 1981-1985.

Consumer Glassware

Artura, #608

This small pattern was manufactured in green, yellow, and pink during the 1930s. It is fairly generic in style with no one distinct feature to distinguish it amongst the many other plain patterns of the time. However, the pattern can be recognized by the nine plain panels which are separated by two thin vertical ribs or lines. The pattern was marketed as a bridge or luncheon set. Good quality examples are difficult to find, making valuation of the items difficult. There are no known reproductions of this pattern.

Item	Green	Pink	Yellow
Creamer	$25	$35	$38
Cup	$15	$22	$28
Plate, salad, 7.5" d	$35	$48	$65
Server, center handle	$35	$75	$100
Saucer	$10	$18	$28
Sherbet, footed	$30	$45	$56
Sugar, open	$25	$35	$38
Tumbler, footed	$42	$52	$64

Artura, creamer, green, $25.00.

Artura, handled sandwich server, yellow, $100.00.

Austrian, #200

This pattern was manufactured by three separate companies. It was first produced by the Indiana Tumbler and Goblet Company until fire destroyed their manufacturing facility. The molds were transferred to the Indiana Glass Company where it was produced from 1904 until about 1907. At a later date, the Federal Glass Company acquired the molds and also produced the pattern. This pattern has also been referred to by many collectors as *Western* and *Paneled Oval Fine Cut*. The Indiana Tumbler and Goblet Company made this pattern in a variety of colors, including crystal, amber, canary yellow, and emerald green. A few pieces were produced by Indiana Tumbler and Goblet Company in experimental colors such as cobalt blue, chocolate, and Nile green. Indiana Glass, however, made this pattern only in crystal.

Prices for some items can be high because of the association with the Indiana Tumbler and Goblet Company. There is no simple way to distinguish the crystal items by manufacturer. However, experienced collectors and appraisers usually look at the clarity of the glass and the overall finishing of the glass. Indiana Tumbler and Goblet Company items usually have a higher degree of clarity and brilliance due to the difference in processing techniques.

Austrian, sugar w/ cover, crystal, $78.00.

Item	Crystal
Banana Stand	$230
Bowl, berry/salad, deep, 8" d	$78
Bowl, berry/salad, shallow, 8" d	$68
Bowl, rectangular, 7.25" l	$88
Bowl, rectangular, 8.75" l	$78
Bowl, rose, small	$88
Bowl, rose, medium	$110
Bowl, rose, large	$130
Bowl, sauce, flat, 4.25" d	$32
Bowl, sauce, flat, 4.5" d	$26
Bowl, sauce, square	$32
Butter w/cover	$260
Cake Stand	$140
Compote, open, high	$96
Compote, open, low	$110
Cordial	$78
Creamer w/cover, 4.5" h	$40
Creamer, large	$88
Creamer, berry, footed	$68
Cup, punch	$26
Goblet	$78
Nappy w/cover, handled	$70
Pitcher, water	$260
Plate, dinner, 10" d	$99
Plate, square	$77
Punch Bowl	$180
Shaker	$68
Spooner	$68
Sugar w/cover, 2.5" d	$53
Sugar w/cover, 4" d	$78
Sugar, berry, footed	$99
Tumbler	$47
Vase, 6" h	$58
Vase, 8" h	$78
Vase, 10" h	$96
Wine	$38

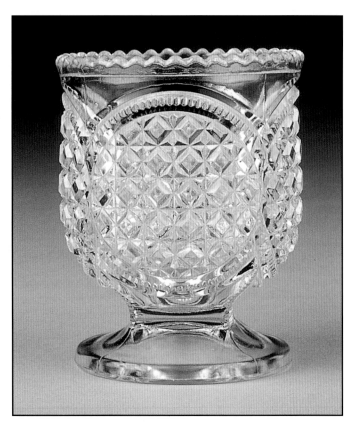

Austrian, spooner, crystal, $68.00.

Avocado, #601

This pattern, most commonly referred to as *Avocado*, is also known as *Sweet Pear* or *Sugar Pear*. It was introduced and manufactured as a luncheon and serving set. The pattern was initially manufactured from 1923 to 1933 in green, pink, and crystal. This pattern is considered by many to be the first true depression glass pattern. That could be debated. However, one thing that cannot be debated is that it ranks as one of the longest running depression glass patterns.

A handful of items in this pattern were reissued yet again through Tiara Exclusives in amethyst (1976), blue, burnt honey (1981), etched crystal, dusty rose (1974), etched coral, etched blue, etched dusty rose, etched lime, etched sunset, etched teal, lime (1985), sunset, teal, and yellow mist (1984). During the 1950s, the pitcher and the tumbler were reissued in milk white. Most items are easily found, but the pitchers and the tumblers demand a fairly high price. It is still up in air whether or not the new colors that Indiana produced will ever demand the prices that the original colors are demanding. Values for the burnt honey and yellow mist colors have been included since there appears to be a good bit of these on the market.

Item	Crystal	Green	Pink	Milk White	Burnt Honey	Yellow Mist
Bowl, berry/salad, 7.5" d	$16	$120	$54	-	-	-
Bowl, berry/salad, 8.5" d	$21	$62	$52	-	-	-
Bowl, berry/salad, 9.5" d	$38	$280	$160	-	-	-
Bowl, preserve, 2-handled, 5.25" d	$12	$40	$50	-	-	-
Bowl, preserve, 1-handle, 7" d	$10	$74	$32	-	-	-
Bowl, relish, footed, 6" d	$10	$41	$32	-	-	-
Bowl, relish, oval, 2-handled, 8.5" l	$18	$38	$49	-	-	-
Creamer, footed	$18	$98	$38	-	$19	$13
Cup, footed, 2-styles	-	$41	$38	-	-	-
Pitcher, 64 oz.	$380	$1600	$1100	$420	$48	$52
Plate, cake, 2-handled, 10.25" d	$18	$170	$130	-	-	-
Plate, luncheon, 8.25" d	$8	$37	$37	-	$12	-
Plate, sherbet, 6.5" d	$6	$23	$17	-	-	-
Saucer, 6.5" d	$6	$26	$34	-	$8	-
Sherbet	-	$78	$65	-	-	-
Sugar, open, footed	$18	$54	$38	-	$18	$17
Tumbler	$38	$340	$210	$45	$10	$20

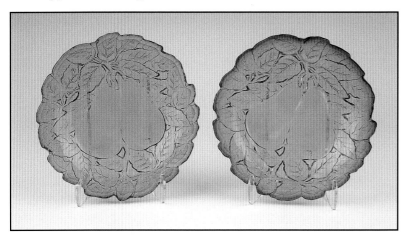

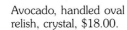

Avocado, pair of saucers, burnt honey, $16.00.

Avocado, handled oval relish, crystal, $18.00.

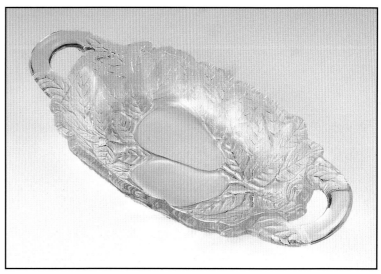

Avocado, luncheon plate, green, $37.00.

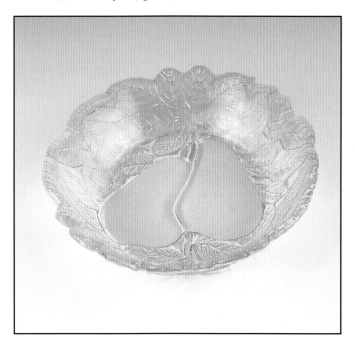

Avocado, round salad bowl, crystal, $16.00.

Beacon Light

This very early pattern began as a Beatty-Brady Glass pattern, circa 1898, and continued in production until about 1904 under the umbrella of the National Glass Company. Items for this pattern are difficult to find making valuation difficult. This pattern can be easily confused with a number of similar patterns such as U.S. Glass's *Shoshone* and Westmoreland's *Sterling*. There are no known reproductions of this pattern.

Item	Crystal
Bowl, berry/salad, 4.5" d	$15
Bowl, berry/salad, 7.5" d	$20
Bowl, berry/salad, 8.5" d	$25
Butter w/cover	$75
Creamer	$35
Cruet w/stopper	$52
Pitcher	$85
Shaker	$60
Spooner	$35
Sugar w/cover	$35
Tumbler	$24

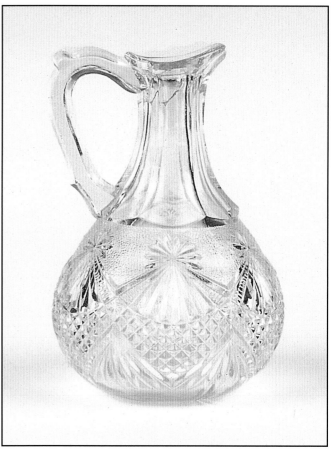

Beacon Light, cruet (w/o stopper), crystal, $20.00.

Bethlehem Star, #152

This pattern can be easily confused with a number of other similar star patterns which were produced at the time such as U.S. Glass's *Starglow* and Lancaster Glass's *Starlyte*. While, many companies produced star pattern glassware, only Indiana produced this pattern in heavy glass with a scalloped edge. Also known as *Bright Star*, this pattern was manufactured from circa 1912 to about 1927. This pattern was made only in undecorated crystal and many of the pieces have a gray tint to the glass. When identifying this pattern, look for the eight-point star and three rays between the points of the star. All the footed items in this pattern have a hexagonal foot and there are no known reproductions of this pattern.

Bethlehem Star, master berry/salad bowl, crystal, $47.00.

Item	Crystal
Bowl, berry/salad, 4.25" d	$13
Bowl, berry/salad, 4.75" d	$13
Bowl, berry/salad, 7.5" d	$26
Bowl, berry/salad, 8.5" d	$47
Bowl, relish, oval, 8.5" l	$17
Bowl, pickle, oval, 10.5" l	$26
Butter w/cover	$88
Celery Vase, handled	$78
Compote, jelly, open, 4.5" d	$64
Compote w/cover, 5.5" d	$68
Compote w/cover, 6.5" d	$99
Creamer	$45
Cruet w/stopper	$57
Goblet	$52
Pitcher, milk, 48 oz.	$68
Pitcher, water, 64 oz.	$99
Spooner, handled	$36
Sugar w/cover	$68
Syrup	$110
Toothpick Holder	$52
Tumbler	$36
Wine	$78

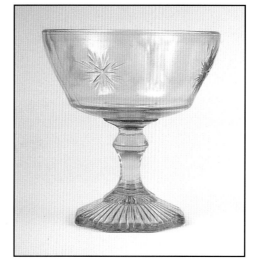

Bethlehem Star, covered compote (w/o cover), crystal, $32.00.

Bethlehem Star, handled spooner, crystal, $36.00.

Bethlehem Star, creamer, crystal, $45.00.

Bird and Strawberry, #157

Sometimes called *Bluebird*, this pattern is quite popular among collectors. This pattern is one of the few Indiana Glass patterns with a wildlife theme. Production for this pattern began circa 1914 and was manufactured in crystal, crystal with colored staining, and goofus. Each item features birds flying amongst strawberry vines with a cane banding around the top and bottom. This pattern is reasonably available in crystal, but is highly sought after when the pieces have been stained. You can effectively double the value of the item when there is good staining present. Some of the harder to find pieces are pitchers, goblets, hats, compotes, and the footed rose bowl. The oval celery tray was reissued in blue from 1980 to 1985 by Indiana and sold through Tiara Exclusives.

Item	Crystal
Bowl, berry/salad, 4.5" d	$32
Bowl, berry/salad, 4-toed, 5" d	$57
Bowl, berry/salad, 7.5" d	$59
Bowl, berry/salad, 9.5" d	$58
Bowl, berry/salad, oval, 4-toed, 9.5" l	$190
Bowl, pickle, oval, 8.5" l	$33
Bowl, celery, oval, 10.5" l	$110
Bowl, relish, heart-shaped	$99
Bowl, sauce	$26
Bowl, serving, 10" d	$140
Bowl, serving, 10.5" d	$70
Butter w/cover	$160
Cake Stand, 9.5" d	$110
Celery Vase	$160
Compote, jelly, open, 4.75" d	$260
Compote w/cover, 5.5" d	$290
Compote w/cover, 6.5" d	$180
Compote, open, ruffled edge, 6" d	$120
Creamer	$88
Cup, custard or punch	$40
Goblet, barrel shape	$570
Goblet, flared shape	$880
Hat	$1900
Pitcher	$340
Plate, salad or dessert, 6.25" d	$230
Plate, serving, 11" d	$180
Plate, chop, 12" d	$210
Spooner	$99
Sugar w/cover	$140
Tumbler	$78
Wine	$90

Bird & Strawberry, covered compote (w/o cover), crystal, $100.00.

Bird & Strawberry, oval relish bowl, blue, $25.00.

Bird & Strawberry, cake stand, $110.00.

Bosc Pear, master berry/salad bowl, crystal w/ gold stain, $33.00.

Bosc Pear, #150

One of the many fruit oriented patterns that Indiana Glass created, this pattern began production circa 1913 and appears to have finished its run by 1917. The pattern was manufactured in crystal, crystal with gold staining, and crystal with colored staining. You could add as much as twenty-five percent for items that have intact gold staining and you can effectively double the value for items that have a good quality colored staining. The pattern was manufactured as a water set, berry set, and breakfast set. There are no known reproductions of this pattern. Be careful not to confuse this pattern with the *Baltimore Pear* pattern, which was manufactured by several companies throughout the years, including Adams & Company, the U.S. Glass Company, and the Jeanette Glass Company.

Item	Crystal
Bowl, berry/salad, 4.5" d	$13
Bowl, berry/salad, 8.5" d	$33
Butter w/cover	$55
Celery Vase	$33
Creamer	$33
Pitcher, water, 64 oz.	$83
Spooner	$33
Sugar	$40
Tumbler	$24

Bosc Pear, creamer & sugar, crystal, $73.00.

Christmas Candy, #624

Similar to the *Ribbon Candy* pattern issued by Bryce Glass in the late 1880s, this pattern began production circa 1954. This pattern was initially produced in crystal and later manufactured in teal. Indiana promoted the teal color as terrace green. Crystal creamers and sugars are plentiful since their production extended into the early 1960s. Production for the rest of this pattern had ended by the late 1950s. Because of the demand for the teal colored items, prices are much higher than they are for crystal. This pattern was produced as a full table set and there are no known reproductions of this pattern.

Item	Crystal	Teal
Bowl, cereal, 5.75" d	$7	-
Bowl, soup, 7.5" d	$12	$78
Bowl, vegetable, 9.5" d	-	$590
Creamer	$16	$40
Cup	$8	$36
Mayonnaise, w/ladle and liner	$25	-
Plate, bread, 6" d	$6	$20
Plate, dinner, 9.5" d	$12	$54
Plate, luncheon, 8.25" d	$16	$32
Plate, sandwich, 11.25" d	$25	$70
Saucer	$5	$16
Sugar, open	$16	$36
Tidbit, 2-tier	$21	$82

Christmas Candy, cup & saucer, crystal, $13.00.

Christmas Candy, creamer & sugar, terrace green, $56.00.

Christmas Candy, luncheon plate, crystal, $16.00.

Constellation, #300

The full line of this pattern began production in the mid-1940s with some items, such as cake stands and goblets, remaining in intermittent production well into the 1990s. The full pattern was manufactured in crystal during the 1940s with certain items being produced in milk white and amber during the 1950s and 1960s. Again, during the 1970s and 1980s certain items in this pattern were manufactured in burnt honey (1980), teal (1980-1981), yellow mist (1982-1983), and sunset (1974-1977) for Tiara Exclusives. I have seen a few items in green, which looks as if it may have been made at the same time as the initial run in crystal.

Crystal items in this pattern are available in a plethora of shapes and sizes and are widely available. Many of the crystal items were produced with a fruit intaglio in the center, of which some intaglios are clear while others are etched. Indiana included this fruit intaglio in several of their patterns. You can add an extra ten percent for this, since these items are not as quite as prevalent as those without the intaglio. Not all items were manufactured in all the colors mentioned earlier. Therefore, if you want to collect a large set you will need to collect the crystal.

Item	Crystal	Sunset	Burnt Honey	Teal	Yellow Mist	Milk White
Basket, handled, 7" h	$24	$76	-	-	$27	$15
Basket, handled, 12" h	$32	$27	$114	$50	$38	$25
Bowl, berry/salad, 8.5" d	$44	-	-	-	-	-
Bowl, berry/salad, 9.5" d	$27	-	-	-	-	-

Item(Cont'd)	Crystal	Sunset	Burnt Honey	Teal	Yellow Mist	Milk White
Bowl, berry/salad, flat, 10" d	$25	-	-	-	-	-
Bowl, berry/salad, flat, 10.5" d	$25	-	-	-	-	-
Bowl, berry/salad, flat, 12.5" d	$25	-	-	-	-	-
Bowl, berry/salad, 3-toed, 5.75" d	$14	-	-	-	-	-
Bowl, berry/salad, 3-toed, 7.5" d	$20	-	-	-	-	-
Bowl, berry/salad, 3-toed, 9.5" d	$22	-	-	-	-	-
Bowl, berry/salad, 3-toed, 11.75" d	$45	-	-	-	-	-
Bowl, mint w/cover, 3-toed, 6.5" d	$24	$30	-	-	$52	$20
Bowl, celery, oval, 10.5" l	$25	-	-	-	-	-
Bowl, mayo, w/ underplate and ladle	$27	-	-	-	-	-
Bowl, nappy, 7.75" d	$18	-	-	-	-	-
Bowl, nappy, 6" d	$18	-	-	-	-	-
Bowl, nut, cupped, 6" d	$11	-	-	$11	$16	$10
Bowl, oval, 2-handled, 11" l	$22	-	-	-	-	$17
Bowl, pickle, 2-handled, 8.5" l	$16	-	-	-	-	-
Bowl, punch, 13.5" d	$38	-	-	-	-	-
Bowl, punch, footed, 12.5" d	$58	-	-	-	-	-
Bowl, relish, 3-part, 12.5" l	$20	-	-	-	-	-
Bowl, relish, 3-part, handled, 6"	$20	-	-	-	-	-
Bowl, rose, 6.5" d	$36	-	-	-	-	-
Cake Stand, round, 10.25" d	$104	-	-	$86	-	$35
Cake Stand, square, 10.25" d	$70	-	-	-	-	$35
Candlestick, 2-lite, 3-styles, pr.	$30	-	-	-	-	-
Candlestick, triangular, 1-lite	$19	-	-	-	$30	-
Claret, 4 oz.	$10	-	-	-	-	-
Cocktail, 3 oz.	$10	-	-	-	-	-
Comport, belled, flat rim, 11.5" d	$27	$38	-	$27	$28	-
Cookie Jar w/cover	$27	-	-	-	-	-
Creamer	$18	-	-	-	-	-
Cup	$16	-	-	-	-	-
Goblet, 8 oz.	$14	$10	-	-	-	$5
Ice Tub, handled, 5.5" d	$45	-	-	-	-	-
Pitcher, 64 oz.	$43	$50	-	-	$27	-
Plate, bread, 7.5" d	$11	-	-	-	-	-
Plate, buffet, 18" d	$32	-	-	-	-	-
Plate, cake, 11" d	$28	-	-	-	-	-
Plate, dessert, 6" d	$5	-	-	-	-	-
Plate, dinner, 9.25" d	$14	-	-	-	-	-
Plate, salad, 8.25" d	$8	-	-	-	-	-
Plate, torte, 14" d	$26	-	-	-	-	-
Platter, oval, 12.5" l	$24	-	-	-	-	-
Salver, 13.5" d	$26	$27	-	$27	$30	-
Saucer	$8	-	-	-	-	-
Sherbet, footed, low	$15	-	-	-	-	-
Sherbet, footed, tall, 4.5 oz.	$25	-	-	-	-	-
Sugar	$11	-	-	-	-	-
Tumbler, 12 oz.	$25	-	-	-	-	-
Tumbler, 8 oz.	$14	-	-	-	-	-
Vase, 3-toed, 8" h	$55	-	-	-	-	-
Vase, swung	$85	-	-	-	-	-
Wine, 2.5 oz.	$10	-	-	-	-	-

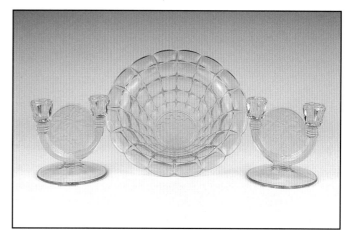

Constellation, console set w/ intaglio, crystal, $57.00.

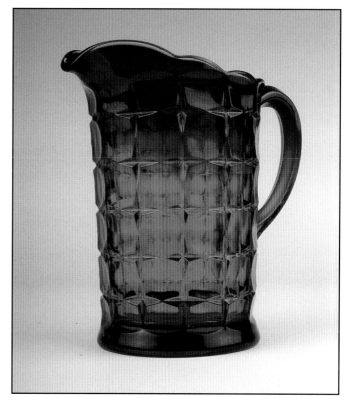

Constellation, water pitcher, sunset, $50.00.

Constellation, footed candy box with cover, crystal, $24.00.

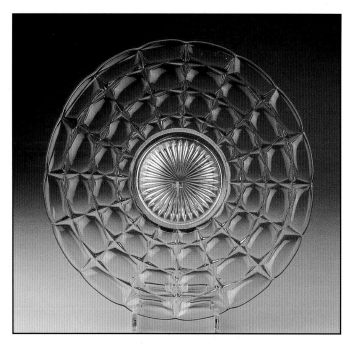

Constellation, serving platter, crystal, $26.00.

Item	Crystal
Compote w/cover, 4.5"	$78
Compote w/cover, 5.5"	$88
Compote w/cover, 6.5"	$83
Compote w/cover, 8.5"	$110
Creamer, 4.25"	$68
Creamer, 4.75"	$70
Cruet w/stopper	$160
Cup, punch or custard	$38
Goblet	$140
Mug, footed	$78
Pitcher, 64 oz.	$110
Shaker	$79
Spooner	$59
Sugar w/cover	$130
Syrup	$180
Toothpick Holder	$130
Tray	$130
Tumbler	$78
Wine	$120

Cord Drapery, #350

This pattern was first produced by the Indiana Tumbler and Goblet Company from 1898 to 1903 and then later manufactured by Indiana Glass from 1904 through 1907. Colored items as well as crystal items appear to have been made at the Greentown plant, but Indiana only made this pattern in crystal. *Cord Drapery* is reasonably available with prices sometimes varying significantly depending on whether the item has been attributed to Greentown Glass or Indiana Glass. Telling the difference between the two can be difficult. However, Indiana's product may be somewhat less clear than the Greentown product due to differences in their manufacturing processes.

Item	Crystal
Bowl, berry/salad, 8" d	$45
Bowl, berry/salad, footed, 6.25" d	$58
Bowl, berry/salad, footed, 8.25" d	$70
Bowl, pickle, oval, 9.5" l	$45
Bowl, rectangular	$77
Bowl, relish, oval, 8.5" l	$77
Bowl, sauce, flat, 4" d	$32
Bowl, sauce, footed, 4" d	$32
Bowl, sauce, flat, 4.25" d	$32
Bowl, sauce, footed, 4.25" d	$32
Butter w/cover, 4.75" d	$100
Butter w/cover, 5.25" d	$79
Cake Plate, low-footed	$92
Cake Stand	$160
Celery Vase	$140

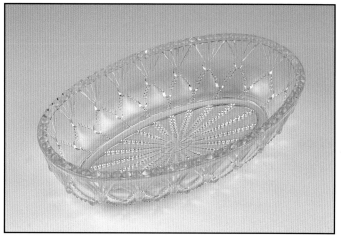

Cord Drapery, oval relish bowl, crystal, $77.00.

Cord Drapery, butter w/ cover, crystal, $79.00.

Cord Drapery, low-footed cake plate, crystal, $92.00.

Cord Drapery, sauce bowl, crystal, $32.00.

Cracked Ice

This pattern was produced during the 1930s in both green and pink. This is a highly desirable pattern, and it is difficult to find pieces that are not damaged. Because this pattern has so many pointed edges, the corners are easily bruised or chipped. The design is very similar to Indiana's *Tea Room* with the addition of a diagonal line in the individual panels. The items in this pattern are somewhat lighter in weight than other Indiana glass products. There are no known reproductions of this pattern.

Item	Pink	Green
Creamer	$62	$68
Plate, 6.5" d	$18	$35
Sherbet	$19	$12
Sugar w/cover	$56	$75
Tumbler	$18	$15

Cracked Ice, sherbet plate, green, $35.00.

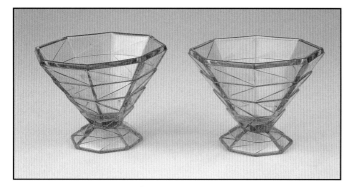

Cracked Ice, pair of footed sherbets, pink, $38.00.

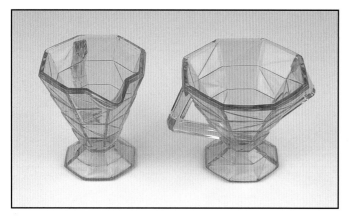

Cracked Ice, creamer & sugar, footed, green, $93.00.

Cracked Ice, tumbler, footed, green, $15.00.

Crystal Ice

This pattern was first introduced in 1980. It was initially manufactured only in crystal, but a few items were manufactured in black, probably for Tiara Exclusives. By 1986, Indiana had warehoused the molds. While collectors may find a few items on the Internet, the best places to find most of these items are at flea markets, second hand shops, and/or thrift stores. While not the hottest collectible pattern at this time, who knows what the future may hold? There are no known reproductions of this pattern.

Crystal Ice, berry/salad bowls, crystal, $25.00.

Item	Crystal
Ash Tray, 8.25" d	$5
Bowl, berry/salad, 5" d	$5
Bowl, berry/salad, 6.75" d	$8
Bowl, berry/salad, 9.5" d	$12
Cake Plate, footed, 11.25" d	$15
Candleholder, pr., 4" h	$10
Cup, soup, 12 oz.	$5
Goblet, 13 oz.	$6
Mug, 15 oz.	$6
Pitcher, 58 oz.	$26
Plate, salad, 7.5" d	$8
Plate, serving, 11.25" d	$12
Sherbet, 8 oz.	$4
Tumbler, 12 oz.	$5
Tumbler, 13 oz.	$5
Wine, 9 oz.	$6

Crystal Ice, handled mug, crystal, $6.00.

Crystal Ice, water pitcher, crystal, $26.00.

Crystal Ice, pair of tumblers, crystal, $6.00.

Crystal Ice, set of tumblers, crystal, $10.00.

Daisy, #620

This very popular pattern had an extremely long production run, making it difficult to classify in any one particular time period. Production on this pattern started during the 1930s and continued well into the 1980s. Relatively few other patterns in the pressed glass genre have enjoyed such longevity. Over the years this pattern was made in amber (1940), crystal (1933), olive green (1960s), milk white (1960s), and fired-on red (1935). This pattern is readily available in amber. It seems to be slightly more difficult to put a collection of the olive green or the milk white together. Crystal grill plates and 7.5" bowls seem to be plentiful, but finding other items in crystal can be a challenge.

Item	Amber/ Red	Crystal/ Olive/ Milk White
Bowl, berry/salad, 4.5" d	$10	$6
Bowl, berry/salad, 7.5" d	$22	$9
Bowl, berry/salad, 9.5" d	$38	$15
Bowl, cereal, 6" d	$32	$11
Bowl, cream soup, 4.5" d	$14	$8
Bowl, relish, 3-part, 8.5" l	$27	$14
Bowl, serving or vegetable, oval, 10" l	$28	$12
Creamer	$13	$21
Cup	$7	$5
Plate, sherbet, 6" d	$9	$8
Plate, salad, 7.5" d	$8	$4
Plate, luncheon, 8.5" d	$12	$6
Plate, dinner, 9.5" d	$10	$8
Plate, grill, 10.5" d	$32	$10
Plate, snack, w/cup indent, 10.5" d		
Plate, serving, 10.75" l	$26	$11
Plate, cake/sandwich, 11.5" d	$31	$15
Saucer	$6	$3
Sherbet	$9	$7
Sugar	$13	$8
Tumbler, 9 oz.	$24	$11
Tumbler, 12 oz.	$43	$22

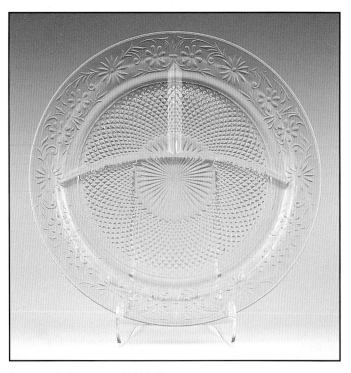

Daisy, grill plate, crystal, $10.00.

Daisy, creamer & sugar, olive green, $29.00.

Daisy, cup & saucer, amber, $13.00.

Daisy and Button with Narcissus, #124

This highly collectible pattern was first introduced circa 1910 in both crystal and crystal with colored staining. Production appears to have been finished by the early 1930s. You can add up to twenty-five percent for items with good quality colored stain. Collectors should be careful as Indiana Glass reissued the decanter and wine glasses during the 1970s, which was sold through Tiara Exclusives. While not one hundred percent reliable, a black light test should be able to distinguish between the old and the new.

Item	Crystal
Bowl, berry/salad, flat, 5" d	$13
Bowl, berry/salad, footed, 5" d	$13
Bowl, berry/salad, 7.25" d	$40
Bowl, berry/salad, 8.25" d	$53
Bowl, berry/salad, oval, footed, 9.25" l	$51
Bowl, celery, oval, 10" l	$32
Bowl, pickle, oval, 9" l	$32
Bowl, olive, leaf shape	$13
Bowl, relish, oval, 8" l	$25
Bowl, sauce, flat, 4" d	$13
Bowl, sauce, footed, 4" d	$13
Butter w/cover	$68
Celery Vase, 3-toed	$53
Compote, jelly, 5" d	$51
Compote, fruit	$79
Compote, low	$45
Creamer	$40
Cup, punch or custard	$20
Decanter w/stopper	$88
Goblet	$47
Pitcher, milk, 32 oz.	$83
Pitcher, water, 64 oz.	$99
Shaker	$59
Spooner	$38
Sugar w/cover	$90
Tray, 10" d	$66
Tumbler	$33
Wine	$33

Daisy & Button w/ Narcissus, footed individual berry/salad bowl, crystal, $13.00.

Daisy & Button w/ Narcissus, oval footed master berry/salad bowl, crystal, $51.00.

Daisy & Button w/ Narcissus, round serving tray, crystal, $66.00.

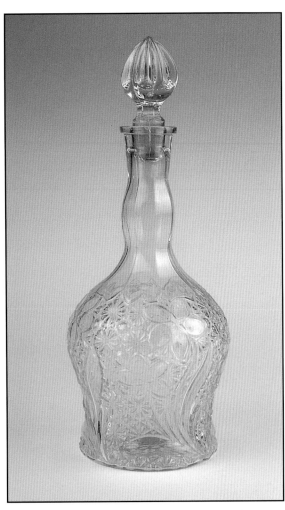

Daisy & Button w/ Narcissus, decanter, crystal, $88.00.

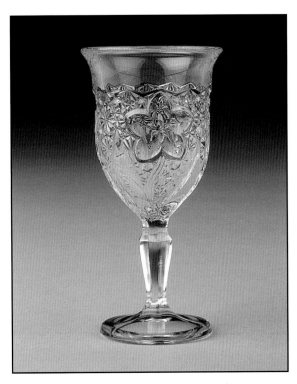

Daisy & Button w/ Narcissus, wine, crystal, $33.00.

Diamond Point

Nearly every item in this pattern was produced in both crystal and crystal with ruby staining. Production of this pattern began in the mid-1960s and continued into the early 1990s. The items made in crystal with ruby staining are more in demand than the plain crystal. Many of the items were produced in amber, amber with gold staining, black, olive green, milk white, etched blue, pastel/ice blue, pastel/ice green, etched pink, pastel pink, and wildfire. I have only included values for the major colors. Diamond Point was issued through Tiara Exclusives in black from 1977 through 1988. Indiana also made Diamond Point in a very pale iridescent gold from 1970 to 1971. All colors of the 15.75" chalice were manufactured with the lid. However, the olive green was never sold with a lid.

Item	Crystal	Crystal w/ Ruby	Amber	Black
Ashtray, 5.5"	$5	-	$4	$8
Basket, applied handle, 13.5"	$24	$42	$16	-
Bowl, berry/salad, flat rim, 5"	$13	$13	$5	$10
Bowl, berry/salad, flat rim, 6"	$8	$12	$5	-
Bowl, berry/salad, scalloped rim, 6"	$6	$14	$8	-
Bowl, berry/salad, straight side, 9.75"	$17	$24	-	$25
Bowl, berry/salad, low foot, scalloped, 11.5"	$16	$25	-	-
Bowl, berry/salad, low foot, flared, 13.25"	$32	$41	$20	-
Bowl, console, oval, 4-toed, 8.5"	$10	$20	$10	-
Bowl, mayonnaise, 3-toed, crimped	$13	$16	$10	-
Bowl, relish, 2-part, 6" d	$8	$12	-	-
Butter w/cover	$27	$33	$20	$30
Cake Stand, 12"	$48	$144	-	-
Candle Lamp, 5.5" h	$11	-	$6	-
Candy Box w/cover, low, boutique, 3.75" d	$14	-	$12	$16
Candy Box w/cover, tall, footed, 7" d	$20	$22	$18	$27
Chalice w/cover, 15.75" h	$27	$28	$15	$31
Compote, 7.5" d	$19	$18	$18	$20
Cup	$6	$13	-	-
Creamer, 6 oz.	$7	$12	$6	$14
Decanter, 24 oz.	$17	$31	-	-
Goblet, 11 oz.	$8	$11	$4	$10
Ice Bucket w/cover, 11.5" h	$21	$35	$41	$43
Ice Bucket, crimped edge, 10" h	$21	$40	-	-
Mug, 10 oz.	$9	$25	-	$7
Pitcher, 65 oz.	$27	$225	$16	$38
Plate, cake/sandwich	$16	42	-	-
Plate, dinner, 9.5" d	$25	$132	-	-
Salt/Pepper	$5	$50	$12	$17
Saucer	$7	$13	-	-
Sherbet, 6 oz.	$5	$10	-	-
Sugar, 9 oz.	$7	$12	$6	$14
Tray, sugar/creamer	$5	$10	$8	$10
Tray, hostess Tray, 12" d	$15	$29	-	-
Tray, relish, 3-part, 12" d	$15	$31	-	-
Tray, relish, 5-part, 12" d	$10	$21	-	-
Tumbler, rocks, 9 oz.	$8	$19	-	$8
Tumbler, water, 12 oz.	$4	$24	-	$5
Tumbler, cooler, 15 oz.	$11	$21	-	$12
Vase, footed, 8"	$17	-	-	-
Wine, 6 oz.	$7	$10	$7	$9

Diamond Point, chalice w/ cover, crystal w/ ruby stain, $28.00.

Diamond Point, set of goblets, olive green & amber, wine, olive green, $4.00, $4.00, & $7.00.

Diamond Point, mug, crystal, $9.00.

Diamond Point, candleholder, amber, $5.00.

Diamond Point, pair of hostess plates, crystal & blue, $15.00 & $18.00.

Diamond Point, pair of serving bowls, crystal & crystal w/ ruby staining, $32.00 & $41.00.

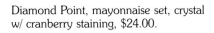

Diamond Point, mayonnaise set, crystal w/ cranberry staining, $24.00.

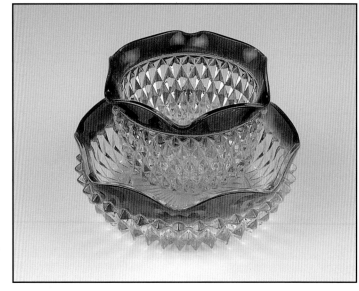

Dogwood, Decorated #9

The blank for this pattern was simply known as #9 and was manufactured as a full service set. Produced in the late 1930s, this pattern was decorated with orange, blue, or green trim where small flowers adorned the banding around the edge of each item. The decoration was hand applied and the end result is a pattern with an art deco flair. There are no known reproductions of this pattern.

Item	Dogwood Decorated
Bowl, berry/salad, 9" d	$20
Bowl, berry/salad, flared, 9.5" d	$20
Bowl, berry/salad, scalloped, 8.25" d	$20
Bowl, mint, covered, heart-shaped, 6.5" d	$15
Bowl, console, rolled edge	$25
Bowl, olive, handled, 6" d	$12
Bowl, relish w/cover, 6.5" d	$12
Bowl, serving w/cover, divided, oval, 8.5" d	$22
Butter Ball tray, center handled, 6" d	$35
Candlestick, low	$24
Cheese dish w/cover, 4.5" d	$15
Comport, low, 9.5" d	$32
Comport, low, 10.75" d	$35
Creamer	$12
Cup	$8
Ice Tub, 6.5" d	$22
Roll Tray, oval, 12" l	$30
Salver, narrow base, 11.5" d	$28
Salver, narrow base, 12.25" d	$28
Salver, wide base, 10.25" d	$28
Salver, wide base, 10.5" d	$28
Sandwich server, center handled, 10.5" d	$32
Sandwich server, center handled, 11.5" d	$32
Saucer	$5
Sugar	$12
Vase, fan-shaped, 8.25"	$24

Dogwood, rolled-edge console bowl, hand-painted, $25.00.

Dogwood, handled sandwich server, hand-painted, $32.00.

Dogwood, flared-edged berry/salad bowl, hand-painted, $20.00.

Double Fleur de Lis, #607

Exact dates for the production of this pattern are difficult to ascertain. We do believe that it was being produced in the late 1940s and probably continued into the early 1950s. Given the pattern number, it may have begun production as early as the late 1930s. This pattern was initially produced in crystal and many items have etchings. Indiana reissued the 3-toed comport through Tiara Exclusives during the early 1980s in cobalt blue. They also created a basket in cobalt blue, which was not part of the initial production of this pattern. As you can see from the list of items, it was sold only as a service set.

Item	Crystal
Bowl, mayonnaise w/plate	$25
Bowl, center, 13.5"	$32
Comport, five shapes, low footed	$38
Comport, five shapes, high footed	$42
Comport, two shapes, 3-toed, 11.5"	$36
Comport, oval, low footed	$22
Creamer	$25
Ice tub, handled	$45
Plate, serving, 15"	$28
Salver, low-footed	$32
Salver, high footed	$38
Sandwich server, center handled, 10"	$32
Sugar, open	$25

Double Fleur de Lis, tri-footed comport, $36.00.

Double Fleur de Lis, low-footed comport, $38.00.

Double Fleur de Lis, creamer, $25.00.

Double Pinwheel

This pattern was issued circa 1904 and continued in production well into the 1920s. *Double Pinwheel* was manufactured in crystal and crystal with gold staining and is relatively easy to collect. This pattern can be distinguished from others by the small pinwheels located on each individual tip of the larger pinwheel. Also known as "Juno," there are no known reproductions of this pattern.

Item	Crystal
Bowl, berry/salad, 7" d	$28
Bowl, berry/salad, 8" d	$36
Bowl, berry/salad, 10" d	$44
Bowl, mint, heart-shaped, 6.25"	$17
Bowl, celery, oval, 10.5" l	$22
Bowl, pickle, oval, 9" l	$23
Bowl, relish, oval, 6" l	$28
Bowl, sauce, 4" d	$17
Bowl, square, 5" w	$25
Bowl, utility, diamond shape, 8.25" d	$35
Butter w/cover	$66
Cake Stand, 9" d	$65
Cake Stand, 10" d	$85
Comport, low-footed	$25
Compote, open, 4" d	$32
Compote, jelly, open, 4.75" d	$38
Compote w/cover, 6" d	$95
Compote w/cover, 7" d	$110
Compote, open, 8" d	$120
Compote, open, 9" d	$150
Creamer, large	$37
Creamer, berry	$37
Cruet w/stopper, 5 oz.	$37
Cup, custard or punch	$25
Goblet	$35
Pitcher, milk, 32 oz.	$86
Pitcher, water, 64 oz.	$100
Plate, dinner, 9"	$75
Shaker	$52

Item(Cont'd)	Crystal
Spooner	$30
Sugar w/cover, large	$44
Sugar, berry, open	$29
Syrup	$110
Toothpick Holder	$33
Tray, condiment, 8.5"	$64
Tumbler	$24
Wine	$35

Double Pinwheel, low-footed comport, crystal, $25.00.

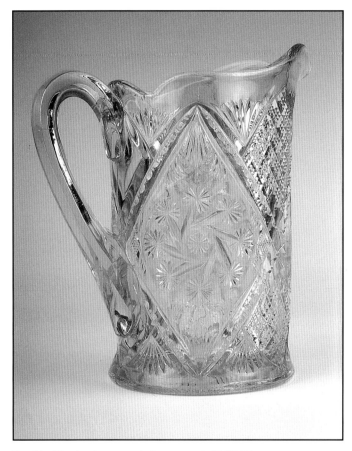

Double Pinwheel, water pitcher, crystal, $100.00.

Double Pinwheel, compote w/ cover, crystal, $95.00.

Double Pinwheel, heart-shaped mint, crystal w/ gold staining, $20.00.

Early American, #170

If there is any one pattern that confounds most collectors, this is the one. Indiana originally named this pattern Early American and it is one of the few patterns that Indiana gave both a name and a number. However, I will refer to it as *Sandwich* since that is the name used by most collectors. The pattern was introduced in the late 1920s and continued in sporadic production until the Dunkirk plant closure. It was made in a wide assortment of colors over the years and enjoyed a spectacular revival during the 1970s and 1980s when it was sold and distributed through Tiara Exclusives.

Today you will find quite a bit of this pattern on the market, especially in the amber color. Its initial production in the late 1920s and early 1930s was mainly in crystal and green with a limited production in amber, pink, and red. However, that does not mean if you have these colored pieces that they are from that time period. Crystal items were manufactured on and off from the 1920s to 1998. The last known round of crystal sandwich was sold through Tiara Exclusives from 1978 to 1998. The chantilly green version of this pattern gets many novices thinking that they have true depression glass. Most of the time, and I emphasize most, a simple black light test will tell the truth. Indiana reissued red in 1970 and amber was produced for twenty years.

While the pattern is easily recognized, it is very often confused with many of the other similar sandwich style patterns that make their way from estates to auctions to new collections. In order to easily distinguish this sandwich pattern from the others, look for the downward sloping feathers. Anchor Hocking's *Sandwich* pattern has feathers that rise. Duncan & Miller's *Sandwich* pattern also has downward sloping feathers, but most pieces have a scalloped edge, which Indiana's does not. On another note, if you have the diamond-shaped creamer, sugar, and tray, these shapes are later issues and were not original to the pattern. The shape was taken from the *Pineapple and Floral* pattern and issued in the early 1950s. Indiana created many newer items when they sold this pattern through Tiara. Items such as the napkin holder, basket, canisters, footed creamers and sugars, coasters, and clocks were not original to the pattern.

As far as colors go, I have already mentioned crystal with regards to production dates. If you have amber (1971-1991), chantilly green (1982-1991), peach (1990-1998), red (1970), bicentennial blue (1976), spruce green (1995-1998) or plum (1999), these were all sold through Tiara Exclusives. The milk white items were made during the late 1950s and early 1960s. A few of the items, mainly the tall handled basket, the jewel box, the candle lamp, and the puff box were issued in the red color until 1985. From the mid- to late 1980s, Indiana manufactured the jewel box in a grey color, which they called platinum.

Item	Crystal	Amber	Red	Chantilly	Peach
Ashtray Set	$15	$14	-	$33	$16
Basket, 10" h	$36	$66	-	$35	-
Bowl, berry/salad, 4.75" d	$7	$5	-	$4	$4
Bowl, berry/salad, scalloped edge, 6" d	$10	-	-	-	-
Bowl, berry/salad, 8.5" d	$12	$30	-	$27	$23
Bowl, celery, oval, 10.5" l	$18	$20	-	-	-
Bowl, console, straight/crimped rim, 9" d					
Bowl, console, belled edge, 11.5" d	$50	$80	-	$50	$54
Bowl, nappy, hexagonal, 6" d	$12	-	-	$12	-
Butter w/cover	$26	$26	-	$38	-
Candlesticks, pair, low, 3.5" h	$21	$19	-	$49	$49
Candlesticks, pair, high, 7" h	$40	$32	-	$48	-
Clock	-	$46	-	$80	$82
Creamer, berry, diamond	$9	$9	-	-	-
Creamer, berry, round	$10	$10	-	-	-
Creamer, large, round	$10	$10	$50	$15	$15
Cruet w/stopper, 6 oz.	$28	$28	-	-	-
Cup	$4	$4	$31	$5	$5
Decanter w/stopper	$26	$26	$94	$35	-
Goblet, water, 9 oz.	$16	$15	$73	$10	$10
Mayonnaise, footed	$15	$15	-	-	-
Pitcher, 68 oz.	$25	$55	$180	$40	$40
Plate, sherbet, 6" d	$4	$4	-	-	-
Plate, bread, 7" d	$5	$5	-	-	-
Plate, luncheon, 8.5" d	$8	$8	$22	$6	$6
Plate, dinner, 10.5" d	$10	$12	-	$18	$12
Plate, sandwich, center handle, 11" d	$21	$21	-	-	-
Plate, cake/sandwich, 13" d	$15	$15	-	-	-
Plate, snack, oval, w/indent, 8" l	$6	$6	-	$10	$10
Puff Box w/cover	$19	$18	-	$10	$10
Salt and Pepper, pair	$19	$19	-	$15	$15
Saucer	$4	$4	$8	$4	$4
Sherbet, 3.25"	$6	$6	-	$5	$5
Sugar, berry, diamond	$9	$9	-	-	-
Sugar, berry, round	$10	$10	-	-	-
Sugar, large, round	$24	$24	$50	$25	$25
Tray, 13" d	$15	$15	-	-	-
Tray, creamer/sugar, handled, 9" l	$15	$15	-	-	-
Tray, wine, 10.5" d	$15	$15	-	$12	$12
Tumbler, footed, cocktail, 3 oz.	$8	$8	-	-	-
Tumbler, footed, water, 8 oz.	$10	$10	-	-	-
Tumbler, footed, iced tea, 12 oz.	$12	$12	-	$10	$10
Wine, 4 oz.	$12	$10	$35	-	-

Early American, luncheon plate, crystal, $8.00.

Early American, open compote, blue, $32.00.

Early American, 8 pc. snack set, amber, $40.00.

Early American, pair of footed tumblers, plum, $20.00.

Early American, creamer & sugar w/ tray, crystal, $33.00.

Early American, candle lamp, amber, $15.00.

Early American, oblong celery bowl, crystal, $18.00.

Early American, bridge set, crystal, amber, chantilly green, $4.00, $4.00, $4.00 & $8.00.

Ferris Wheel

Introduced circa 1909, this pattern was manufactured in crystal and crystal with gold staining. Also known as *Prosperity* and *Lucile*, this pattern has begun to catch the eye of newer collectors. If you want to assemble a full set, you will need to be patient. The items are out there but it will take some time to find them. This pattern was manufactured until about 1915.

This pattern is often confused with Westmoreland's *Paddlewheel Shield*, which was being produced about the same time. The clarity of the glass is average to good on most pieces. Both of the known compotes in this pattern are covered. The cake stand seems to be readily available.

Item	Crystal
Bowl, berry/salad, flat, 4" d	$15
Bowl, berry/salad, flat, 6.5" d	$40
Bowl, preserve, leaf-shape, 7.5" l	$22
Butter w/cover	$72
Cake Stand, 9" d	$66
Celery Vase	$53
Compote w/cover, high, 5.25" d	$39
Compote w/cover, low, 7.5" d	$79
Creamer, berry,	$40
Creamer, large, flat	$40
Cruet w/stopper, 5 oz.	$46
Goblet	$33
Pitcher, milk, 32 oz.	$73
Pitcher, water, 64 oz.	$88
Shaker	$59
Spooner	$33
Sugar w/cover, large, flat	$53
Sugar, berry, open	$33
Tumbler	$33
Vase, 6.25"	$40
Wine	$33

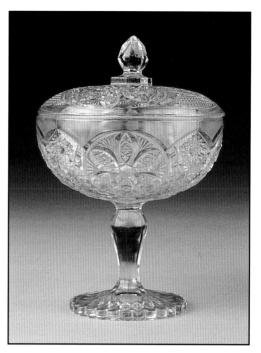

Ferris Wheel, compote w/ cover, crystal, $39.00.

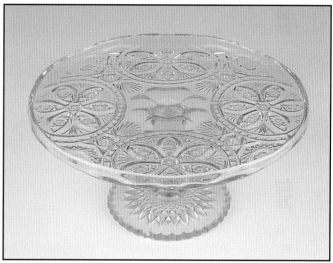

Ferris Wheel, high-footed cake stand, crystal, $66.00.

Ferris Wheel, berry sugar, crystal w/ gold staining, $33.00.

Ferris Wheel, berry/salad bowl, crystal, $40.00.

Flower Medallion, #158

Issued as early as 1915, *Flower Medallion* or *Eclipse* as it has also been called, is primarily found in crystal and widely available. If you prefer gold stained items, you can assemble a collection of those with a little more effort. While scarce, you can also find items with red, green, and blue staining. This pattern appears to have been manufactured until about 1924.

Several items in this pattern were reissued by Indiana Glass and offered through Tiara Exclusives. In the late 1970s the pitcher, goblets, and a small compote or wine were reissued in lime green carnival glass and offered as incentives to Tiara hostesses. These Tiara items are hard to find and can demand a high price.

The overall quality of the glass used for this pattern is very good. The clarity is much better than some of Indiana's other patterns. There is not much of a difference in price between items that are all crystal and those with gold staining. However, you can add an additional twenty-five percent for items that have good colored staining. There are no known reproductions of this pattern.

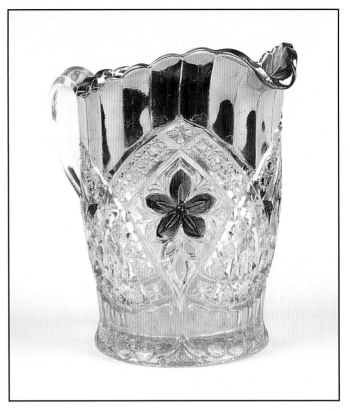

Flower Medallion, creamer, crystal w/ multicolored staining, $74.00.

Item	Crystal
Bowl, berry/salad, 4-toed, 4.5" d	$20
Bowl, berry/salad, flat, 5" d	$20
Bowl, berry/salad, 4-toed, 7.5" d	$46
Bowl, berry/salad, flat, 9" d	$46
Bowl, berry/salad, flat, 10" d	$46
Bowl, relish, oval, 8.5" l	$26
Bowl, celery, oval, 10.5" l	$53
Butter w/cover	$79
Celery Vase	$66
Compote, jelly, open	$40
Creamer	$59
Goblet	$13
Pitcher, 64 oz.	$110
Spooner	$59
Sugar w/cover	$79
Toothpick Holder	$59
Tumbler, 8 oz.	$53

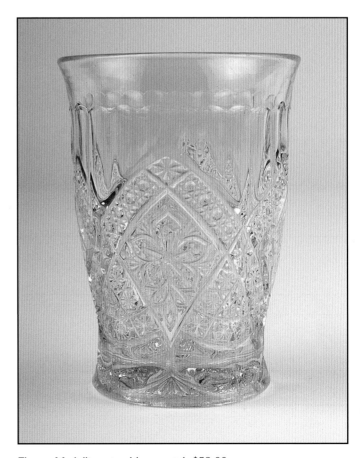

Flower Medallion, tumbler, crystal, $53.00.

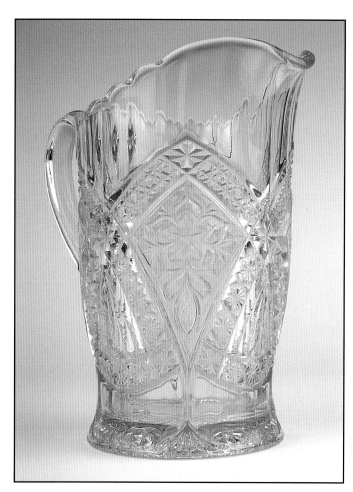

Flower Medallion, water pitcher, crystal, $110.00.

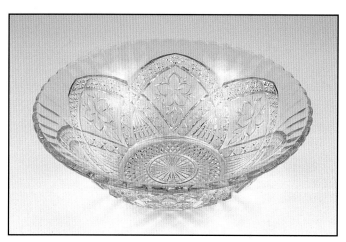

Flower Medallion, master berry/salad bowl, crystal, $46.00.

Gaelic, #168

Production of this pattern began circa 1908 and it was manufactured in crystal, crystal with gold staining, and crystal with colored staining. The pattern was manufactured until about 1931. This pattern is often confused with *Garden Pink* and *Horsemint*, two other flora style patterns. However, knowing that *Gaelic* has one flower per panel, *Horsemint* has two flowers per panel, and *Garden Pink* has three flowers per panel, should help distinguish between the three patterns. You can add approximately twenty-five percent to the value of items that have good quality colored staining. There are no known reproductions of this pattern.

Item	Crystal
Bowl, berry/salad, flat, 4.25" d	$13
Bowl, berry/salad, 3-toed, 5.5" d	$22
Bowl, berry/salad, flat, 7.5" d	$26
Bowl, celery, 10.5" l	$25
Bowl, mint, heart-shaped	$23
Bowl, pickle, 8.5" l	$13
Butter w/cover	$46
Cake Stand, 7.5" d	$42
Cake Stand, 9.25" d	$52
Celery Vase	$26
Compote w/cover, 4.75" d	$40
Compote, jelly, open, 4.75" d	$26
Creamer	$33
Cruet w/stopper	$45
Cup, punch/custard	$26
Goblet	$40
Honey dish w/cover	$65
Pitcher, 64 oz.	$52
Plate, square, mint	$15
Spooner	$30
Sugar	$44
Tray, oval	$15
Tumbler	$27
Wine	$35

Gaelic, open compote, crystal, $26.00.

Gaelic, honey dish, crystal, $65.00.

Gaelic, oval tray, crystal, $15.00.

Gaelic, round footed individual berry/salad bowl, crystal, $22.00.

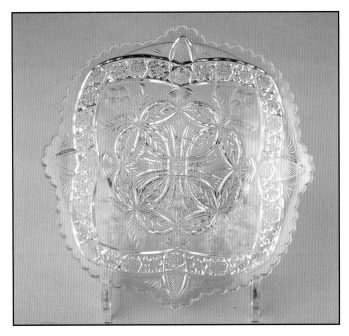

Gaelic, cruet (w/o stopper), crystal, $20.00.

Gaelic, square mint plate,
crystal, $15.00.

Garden Pink, #167

Indiana Glass began producing this pattern circa 1913. As with many of the other Indiana floral patterns, you can find this in crystal, crystal with gold staining, and crystal with gold and colored staining. The pattern is often confused with *Gaelic* and *Horsemint*. However, knowing that *Gaelic* has one flower per panel, *Horsemint* has two flowers per panel, and *Garden Pink* has three flowers per panel, should help distinguish between the three patterns. You can add approximately twenty-five percent to the value of items that have good quality colored staining. There are no known reproductions of this pattern.

Garden Pink, spooner, crystal, $44.00.

Item	Crystal
Bowl, berry/salad, 3-toed, 4.25" d	$29
Bowl, berry/salad, 4-toed, 5.5" d	$44
Bowl, berry/salad, 4-toed, 7.5" d	$46
Bowl, berry/salad, oval, 4-toed, 9.5" l	$40
Bowl, mint, heart-shaped	$29
Bowl, nappy, handled, 5.5" d	$29
Bowl, pickle, oval, 8.5" l	$29
Butter w/cover	$64
Cake Stand	$74
Compote w/cover, 6.5" d	$74
Compote w/cover, 8.5" d	$89
Compote, jelly, open, 4.75" d	$37
Creamer	$35
Goblet	$40
Honey dish w/cover	$52
Pitcher	$86
Spooner	$44
Sugar	$52
Tray, 8.5" d	$18
Tumbler	$37
Wine	$37

Garden Pink, berry/salad set, crystal, $162.00.

Garden Pink, berry/salad bowl, crystal, $44.00.

Garland, #301

Fruit has long been used as a pattern in glassware. Whether it is grapes, pears, apples, or a mixture of the above, fruit has held a long-standing popularity amongst glass collectors. Similar to numerous other fruit patterns produced by Westmoreland and Duncan and Miller, Indiana Glass decided to include bananas in this fruit pattern. As a result, this pattern has earned the nickname, *Banana Fruits*. This pattern was introduced as early as 1935 with many of the items being produced as late as the 1980s. This pattern was predominantly made in crystal with stained fruit, but many of the items were entirely stained or etched. Some pieces in this pattern had the fruit portion of the glass stained in orange, rose or wisteria. The values listed below are for those items that are crystal with the individual fruit stained in multi-colors.

The large oval footed bowl is extremely common and was made in a wide assortment of colors including crystal ($19), olive green ($13), green ($16), amber ($18), milk white ($16), gold iridescent ($21), blue iridescent ($24), green iridescent ($27), red decorated ($18), blue ($20), and pink ($17). While available, the basket, bowls, and platters do not seem to be quite as prevalent. The latter items are not seen too often and most folks are unsure of what they have.

Garden Pink, creamer, $35.00.

Item	Crystal w/staining
Basket, handled, 10.25" h	$44
Bowl, berry/salad, 5.5" d	$16
Bowl, berry/salad, 6" d	$20
Bowl, berry/salad, 7.75" d	$25
Bowl, fruit, oval, 4-toed, 12.25" l	$18
Bowl, rose, 8.25" d	$28
Candlesticks, 2-lite, pr.	$30
Comport, low, 9" d	$22
Comport, low, 10" d	$25
Comport, low, 10.5" d	$24
Comport, low, 11.25" d	$32
Comport, low, 12.25" d	$35
Plate, luncheon, 7.5" d	$20
Plate, dinner, 9.5" d	$25
Salver, 12.5"	$20
Salver, 13"	$24

Garland, oval footed center/ fruit bowl, light green, $16.00.

Garland, low-footed console bowl, crystal w/ multicolored stain, $35.00.

Garland, berry/salad bowl, crystal w/ multicolored stain, $20.00.

Garland, double candlestick, crystal w/ multicolored stain, $15.00.

Gothic Windows, #166

This pattern was produced in crystal and crystal with gold staining from about 1925 through 1930. Also known as *Gothic Arches*, it can be somewhat difficult to locate undamaged pieces. No matter what the condition, the pattern is very sharp, suggesting a brief production period. Many molds used over a long period of time create a mottled effect on the pattern. This pattern is easily recognizable by its graceful gothic style arches. There are no known reproductions of this pattern.

Item	Crystal
Bowl, berry/salad, 4.25" d	$15
Bowl, berry/salad, 4.75" d	$15
Bowl, berry/salad, 3-toed, 5.5" d	$27
Bowl, berry/salad, 6" d	$37
Bowl, berry/salad, belled, 6.5" d	$30
Bowl, berry/salad, crimped, 6.5" d	$30
Bowl, berry/salad, 8.5" d	$35
Bowl, berry/salad, 9" d	$44
Bowl, pickle, oval, 8.5" l	$23
Butter w/cover	$75
Compote w/cover, 4.75" d	$30
Compote w/cover, 5.5" d	$74
Creamer	$37
Goblet	$52
Honey dish w/cover	$86
Pitcher	$98
Spooner	$30
Sugar w/cover	$44
Tumbler	$27

Gothic Windows, butter w/ cover, crystal, $75.00.

Gothic Windows, berry/salad bowl, crystal, $15.00.

Gothic Windows, berry/salad set, crystal, $104.00.

Harvest

Colony Glass, a subsidiary of Lancaster Glass Corporation, designed the very familiar *Harvest* molds sometime around the late 1940s. When Lancaster Glass bought Indiana Glass in 1957, many of the molds were sent to Indiana Glass in Dunkirk to increase production. Both Colony Glass and Indiana Glass produced *Harvest* pattern milk glass items although all of the milk glass items continued to be marketed under the Colony name. Indiana Glass produced this pattern until the demand for milk glass waned in the late 1960s.

The early 1970s saw another trend in American tastes taking place throughout the country. A noticeable increase in the interest of carnival glass had been occurring and Indiana Glass stopped producing this pattern in milk glass and began producing it in iridescent blue, iridescent green, and iridescent gold. The appeal of this new carnival glass was amazing to say the least.

There was some limited production of the vases and canisters in amber and olive green, mostly for the florist trade. However, the primary focus was on producing the carnival glass. Iridescent green seems to demand the higher prices, with iridescent blue following close behind, and iridescent gold running in third. Items in blue and gold are much more prevalent due to their longer production runs.

Harvest, pair of covered compotes, milk white, $20.00.

Harvest, footed vase, olive green, $10.00.

Item	Milk White	Blue	Gold	Green
Bowl, cereal, 6"	$50	-	-	-
Bowl, serving, oval, 9.5" l	$120	-	-	-
Butter w/cover	$87	$42	-	-
Candleholder, 4", pr.	$15	$30	$28	$42
Candy Box, covered, round	$25	$50	$36	$50
Canister, 7"	$68	$27	$27	$38
Canister, 8"	$70	$100	$62	$63
Canister, 9"	$78	$260	$160	$180
Compote, open, 10" d	$16	$28	$22	-
Compote w/cover, 6.5" d	$10	$26	$16	-
Compote w/cover, 7.5" d	$15	$34	$28	-
Creamer	$8	$14	-	$15
Cup	$3	-	-	-
Goblet, 9 oz.	$7	$12	$9	$15
Pitcher, water, 70 oz.	$28	$44	$36	$60
Plate, 8", bread	$25	-	-	-
Plate, 9.75", dinner	$11	-	-	-
Platter, 14", round	$22	-	-	-
Punch Set	$160	-	-	-
Salt/Pepper	$41	-	-	-
Saucer, 6.25"	$3	-	-	-
Sherbet, 3.25"	$8	-	-	-
Snack Set	$23	-	-	$152
Sugar	$8	$14	-	$15
Tray, creamer/sugar	$8	$14	-	$15
Tumbler, 14 oz.	$8	$17	$11	$34
Tumbler, 7.5"	$15	-	-	-
Vase, 10"	$15	-	-	-
Vase, 12"	$22	-	-	-

Harvest, water pitcher, iridescent blue, $44.00.

Harvest, set of four tumblers, iridescent gold, $44.00.

Harvest, canister w/ cover, iridescent gold, $27.00.

Harvest, open compote, milk white, $16.00.

Horsemint, #156

This is another flower pattern similar in many respects to *Gaelic* and *Garden Pink*. However, while *Gaelic* has only one flower per panel and *Garden Pink* has three flowers per panel, *Horsemint* has two flowers per panel. This pattern was produced in crystal and goofus from 1917 to about 1931. Out of all the flowered patterns that Indiana Glass issued, this appears to be the most prevalent, probably because of the number of years it was produced. There are no known reproductions of this pattern.

Item	Crystal
Bowl, banana, footed	$52
Bowl, berry/salad, 3-toed, 4.5" d	$17
Bowl, berry/salad, 10" d	$44
Bowl, mint, heart-shaped	$23
Bowl, cabarette	$35
Bowl, celery, oval, 10.5" l	$27
Bowl, nappy, handled, 5.5" d	$23
Bowl, pickle, oval, 8.5" l	$25
Butter w/cover	$69
Cake Stand	$54
Celery Vase	$37
Compote w/cover, 6.5" d	$74
Compote, open, 7.5" d	$65
Creamer	$37
Goblet	$52
Pitcher, water, 64 oz.	$98
Plate, serving, 12"	$40
Spooner	$30
Sugar w/cover	$44
Tumbler	$37
Vase, footed, 6.5"	$35
Wine	$25

Horsemint, water pitcher, crystal, $98.00.

Horsemint, oval relish bowl, crystal, $27.00.

Horsemint, individual berry/salad bowl, footed, crystal, $17.00.

Horseshoe, #612

This pattern began production in 1930 and ran until 1933. Produced primarily in green and yellow, there are only a few items known in pink and crystal. The gem in this pattern is the butter and cover. Not too many of these surface and, as a result, the value is astronomically high. You will notice that the plates have two different centers. Some are plain, while others have a pattern. There is no significant difference in the values between the plate designs. This pattern was never reissued and there are no known reproductions.

Horseshoe, creamer & sugar, green, $50.00.

Item	Green	Yellow
Bowl, berry/salad, 4.5" d	$69	$27
Bowl, berry/salad, 7.5" d	$44	$43
Bowl, berry/salad, 8.5" d	$44	$38
Bowl, berry/salad, 9.5" d	$133	$98
Bowl, cereal, 6.5" d	$32	$43
Bowl, relish, footed, 3-part	$32	$49
Bowl, serving or vegetable, oval, 10.5" l	$32	$36
Butter w/cover	$1000	-
Candy, in metal holder, motif on lid	$211	-
Creamer, footed	$30	$24
Cup	$19	$18
Pitcher, 64 oz.	$320	$380
Plate, grill, 10.5" d	$135	$250
Plate, luncheon, 9.5" d	$17	$18
Plate, salad, 8.5" d	$29	$29
Plate, sandwich, 11.5" d	$28	$32
Plate, sherbet, 6" d	$28	$28
Platter, oval, 10.75" l	$52	$52
Saucer	$6	$7
Sherbet	$19	$19
Sugar, open	$20	$22
Tumbler, flat, 9 oz.	$190	-
Tumbler, flat, 12 oz.	$190	-
Tumbler, footed, 9 oz.	$36	$36
Tumbler, footed, 12 oz.	$180	$200

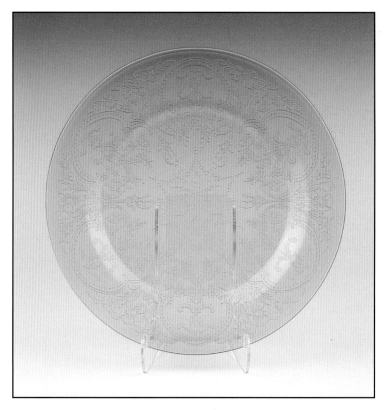

Horseshoe, sandwich/cake plate, green, $28.00.

Horseshoe, master berry/salad bowl, yellow, $38.00.

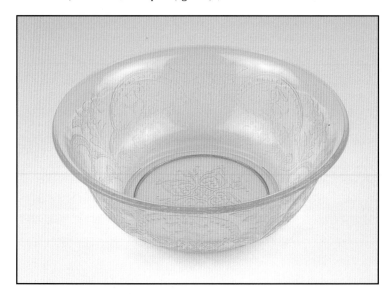

Indiana Custard, #619

Initially I was unsure how to list this pattern. Many other authors and experts on collectible glassware have listed *Indiana Custard* and *Orange Blossom* separately based on the color and the period in which they were produced. In the end, I chose to list them as one in the same. Originally Indiana Custard was produced in the early 1930s in a rich custard or ivory color. Indiana decided to reissue a portion of the items as a luncheon set during the 1950s in milk white, renaming the pattern Orange Blossom. This pattern is also known as *Flower Leaf and Band*.

Item	Custard	Milk White
Bowl, berry/salad, 5.5" d	$24	$8
Bowl, berry/salad, 9" d	$41	-
Bowl, cereal, 6.5" d	$32	-
Bowl, flat soup, 7.5" d	$50	-
Bowl, oval vegetable, 9.5" l	$42	-
Butter w/cover	$74	-
Creamer	$20	$5
Cup	$42	$20
Plate, bread/butter, 5.75" d	$8	$4
Plate, dinner, 9.75" d	$35	-
Plate, luncheon, 9" d	$22	$10
Plate, salad, 7.5" d	$22	-
Platter, oval, 11.5" l	$44	-
Saucer	$14	$8
Sherbet	$110	-
Sugar w/cover	$40	$10

Indiana Custard, luncheon plate, custard, $22.00.

Orange Blossom, creamer & sugar, milk white, $10.00.

Indiana Custard, butter w/ cover, custard, $74.00.

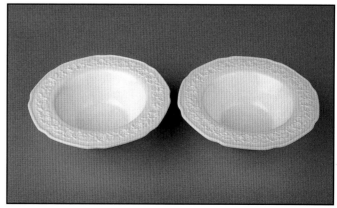

Orange Blossom, pair of individual berry/salad bowls, milk white, $16.00.

Indiana Feather

While known by a wide variety of names, there appears to be two distinct patterns. One pattern, made by the McKee Glass Company and known as Doric, was made in the late 1890s. Indiana Glass, known at the time as National Glass, manufactured Indiana Feather between 1900 and 1906. Cambridge Glass Company also produced this pattern about the same period. McKee made some of the items in green and crystal with an amber stain, but Beatty-Brady made items only in crystal. There are a few ways to tell the difference between the two patterns. The McKee version of this pattern has scalloped rims and a flower type pattern on the bottom of the items, while the Indiana version has straight rims and a star pattern on the bottom. In addition, the Beatty-Brady version has straighter panels with less of a swirl. This pattern is also known as *Finecut and Feathers*.

Item	Crystal
Banana, flat	$110
Banana, footed	$140
Bowl, berry/salad, 6"	$36
Bowl, berry/salad, 7"	$58
Bowl, berry/salad, 8"	$58
Bowl, berry/salad, 9"	$58
Bowl, mint, square, 8"	$64
Bowl, celery, oval, 9.25"	$28
Bowl, pickle, oval, 8.5"	$36
Bowl, sauce, 4"	$22
Bowl, sauce, 4.5"	$22
Bowl, sauce, footed, 4.5"	$22
Bowl, sauce, footed, 4"	$22
Bowl, sauce, square, 4.5"	$36
Bowl, sauce, square, 4"	$36
Butter w/cover	$90
Cake Stand, 8" d	$88
Cake Stand, 10" d	$72
Cake Stand, 11" d	$120
Celery Vase, handled	$74
Champagne	$120
Cheese dish	$210
Compote w/cover, high, 6"	$130
Compote w/cover, high, 7"	$130
Compote w/cover, high, 8"	$180
Compote w/cover, high, 9"	$180
Compote w/cover, high, 10"	$180
Compote w/cover, low, 6"	$130
Compote w/cover, low, 7"	$130
Compote w/cover, low, 8"	$180
Compote w/cover, low, 9"	$180
Compote, jelly, 4.25"	$44
Compote, low, open, 6"	$46
Compote, low, open, 7"	$58
Compote, low, open, 8"	$130
Cordial	$180
Creamer	$68
Cruet w/stopper	$74
Goblet	$78
Honey, round, 3.5"	$22

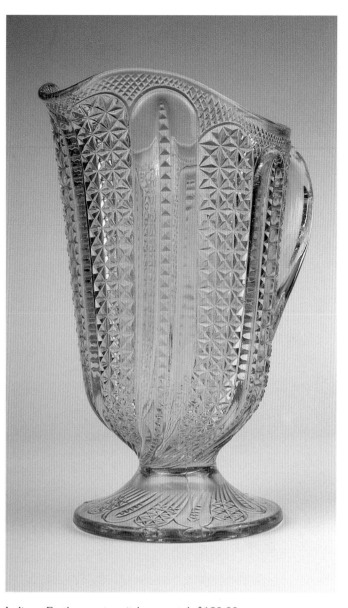

Indiana Feather, water pitcher, crystal, $120.00.

Item	Crystal
Marmalade w/cover	$140
Pitcher, milk, 32 oz.	$72
Pitcher, water, 64 oz.	$120
Plate, bread, 7.75"	$40
Plate, cake or serving	$180
Plate, luncheon, 9.25"	$64
Plate, dinner, 10"	$76
Plate, salad, 8.5"	$60
Relish Tray	$30
Shaker	$90
Spooner	$68
Sugar w/cover	$90
Syrup	$180
Toothpick Holder	$130
Tumbler	$78
Vase	$58
Wine	$68

Indiana Silver, #151

This pattern was first produced circa 1913 and manufactured until about 1918. The pattern was produced in crystal with silver staining. It appears that this pattern was made as a water set, breakfast set, and serving set. The pattern is easily distinguishable by the band of silver flowers at the rim of every item. Items with good quality silver staining are often difficult to find. There are no known reproductions of this pattern.

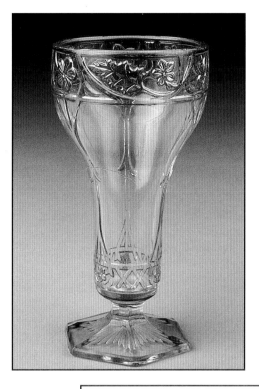

Indiana Silver, footed vase, $26.00.

Item	Crystal
Bowl, berry/salad, 4.25" d	$18
Bowl, berry/salad, 8.25"	$52
Bowl, mint, 3-toed, 5.25" d	$18
Bowl, rose, footed	$40
Butter w/cover	$86
Compote, jelly, open	$40
Creamer, berry	$30
Creamer, large	$30
Goblet	$64
Pitcher, water, 64 oz.	$76
Sherbet	$24
Spooner	$28
Sugar w/cover	$40
Sugar, berry	$40
Tumbler	$22
Vase, 6.5", footed	$26

Indiana Silver, 3-toed mint bowl, $18.00.

Indiana Silver, pair of footed sherbets, crystal w/ silver stain, $48.00.

Jeweled Butterflies

Indiana Glass began production of this pattern around 1907. Produced only in crystal, this pattern was made as a water set, breakfast set, and serving set. *Late Butterfly* and *Mikado* are other names that are used in collecting circles when referring to this pattern. Most pieces are difficult to find, indicating that it may have been produced for just a short period of time. There are no known reproductions of this pattern.

Item	Crystal
Bowl, berry/salad, 5" d	$17
Bowl, berry/salad, 6" d	$52
Bowl, berry/salad, 7" d	$52
Bowl, berry/salad, 8" d	$40
Bowl, relish, oval, 8" l	$30
Bowl, low, 9" d	$59
Bowl, mint, square	$30
Butter w/cover	$89
Creamer, berry	$67
Creamer	$67
Cruet w/stopper	$75
Cup, punch or custard	$30
Pitcher, milk	$120
Pitcher, water	$120
Shaker	$89
Spooner	$67
Sugar w/cover	$89
Sugar, berry, open	$44
Tumbler	$59

Jeweled Butterflies, oval relish bowl, crystal, $30.00.

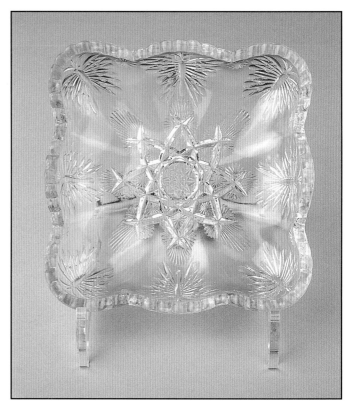

Jeweled Butterflies, square mint bowl, crystal, $30.00.

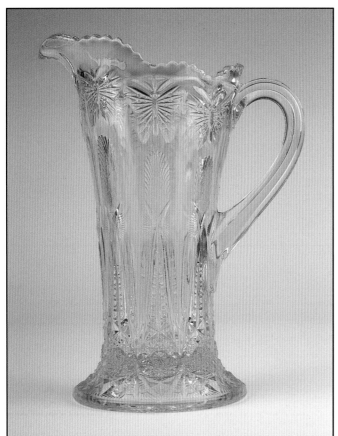

Jeweled Butterflies, milk pitcher, crystal, $120.00.

Killarney, #8

A lot of collectors include this pattern with the *Narcissus Spray* pattern. It is not. Early catalogs have this pattern listed under a different number, precluding it from being a part of the *Narcissus Spray* (#162) pattern. The pattern has been given the name *Killarney* by collectors because of its similarity to the Celtic cross. This appears to be an early pattern given the pattern number. However, if you have this pattern in amber, olive green or iridescent gold, they were manufactured from the 1960s through the late 1980s. Although I am unsure of exactly when this pattern went into initial production, I suspect that it was initially made only in crystal. However, Indiana reissued this pattern in crystal a number of times from the late 1950s through the late 1980s.

If you are collecting this pattern, you should be aware that changes were made to at least some of the molds over the years. Early pressings have a serrated edge as you can see in the photo below. Indiana smoothed the edge at some point, most likely to reduce the chance of chipping. In addition, later issues have a closed handle. Early issues have an open handle. Last but not least, on the newer pressings the divider in the sectional dishes is not as tall as the earlier pressings. As a result, the later pressings are not as well defined as early pressings.

Given the items that I have seen, I expect that this pattern was produced strictly as a service set. I have not seen any pitchers or tumblers, only serving items. If anyone has items other than what is listed please let me know.

Killarney, handled nappy, crystal, $18.00.

Killarney, oval handled sauce bowl, frosted, $15.00.

Killarney, pair of handled divided relishes, crystal & iridescent gold, $22.00 & $18.00.

Item	Crystal	Olive Green	Iridescent Gold	Amber
Bowl, relish, handled	$22	$13	$18	$12
Bowl, relish, divided, handled	$22	$13	$18	$12
Bowl, nappy, handled	$18	-	-	-
Bowl, sauce, oval, handled	$15	-	-	-
Tray, sandwich, handled, 10"	$16	-	-	-

King's Crown, #77

It is a misconception among many collectors that Indiana Glass began producing this pattern after the closure of the Tiffin, Ohio, factory of U.S. Glass. Catalogs from Indiana Glass show this pattern being manufactured well before the closure of Tiffin.

This pattern was originally conceived as *Excelsior* and manufactured by Adams & Co. Glass in the 1880s. The pattern then continued in production through U. S. Glass in the 1890s and early 1900s. This pattern was so popular that several companies made "knock offs" or imitations. Indiana was one of those companies. Given the pattern number (#77), Indiana's version of *King's Crown* must have made its debut early. However, it appears that they only produced various size stems. It was most certainly made in crystal, but was probably made in crystal with ruby staining as well.

In the mid- to late 1950s Indiana Glass was producing these stems in crystal and crystal with ruby staining and cranberry staining. By the mid-1960s, Indiana was producing this pattern in amber, olive green, smoky blue, and milk white, as well as crystal with ruby, cranberry, yellow, gold, and platinum staining. When Indiana acquired the U.S. Glass version of these molds, they were retooled and incorporated into Indiana's molds. Indiana continued to produce this pattern into the 1990s in a variety of colors. The last color for this pattern was imperial blue, which was put into production in 1986 and continued in production until 1995. The compotes were manufactured in many colors including carnival and mass-marketed as wedding bowls and candy bowls. Many of these items were sold through the florist industry.

If you want to collect a complete set you will have to collect the crystal with ruby staining. Not every item was produced in the other colors. If you do not see your item listed in this book, most likely it was an item produced by Tiffin and not by Indiana Glass.

Item	Crystal w/Ruby	Amber	Olive Green
Bowl, berry/salad, 9" d	$92	-	-
Bowl, dessert, 4"	$30	$12	$15
Bowl, fruit, flared, footed, 10.25" d	$150	$19	$22
Bowl, wedding or candy, footed, 5" d	$22	$14	$14
Bowl, wedding or candy, with cover, footed, 5"d	$32	$19	$22
Bowl, wedding or candy, footed, 7" d	$81	-	-
Cake Stand, 12" d	$120	-	-
Candlesticks, sherbet-style, 3.75" d, pr.	$32	-	-
Candlesticks, hand bell-style w/prisms, 8.5" h, pr.	$75	-	-
Creamer	$25	$7	$10
Cup	$11	-	-
Pitcher	$220	-	-
Plate, dinner, 10.25" d	$65	-	-
Plate, cake or serving, 13.5" d	$88	$30	$35
Plate, salad, 8.25" d	$22	$8	$12
Platter, serving, 10.5"	$		
Platter, relish, 5-part, 13.75" d	$140		-
Saucer, 6" d	$12	-	-
Sherbet, 3.75" d	$10	$5	$8
Snack set, 8-pieces	$45	$25	$30
Stem, claret, 4 oz.	$15	$8	$13
Stem, cocktail, 2.5 oz.	$14	-	-
Stem, cordial, 2 oz.	$15	-	-
Stem, goblet, 7.5 oz.	$17	$13	$14
Stem, wine, 5 oz.	$18	$14	$15
Sugar, open	$25	$7	$10
Tidbit, 2-tier, 10" h	$180	-	-
Tidbit, 3-tier, 14" h	$200	-	-
Tumbler, iced tea, 2-styles	$22	$8	$10

King's Crown, set four of footed sherbets, crystal w/ yellow stain, $40.00.

King's Crown, pair of compotes, olive green w/ cover & blue w/o cover, $22.00 & $18.00.

King's Crown, goblets, crystal, crystal w/ ruby stain & olive green, $10.00, $17.00, & $14.00.

King's Crown, compote, crystal w/ platinum stain, $35.00.

King's Crown, sauce/dessert bowl, crystal w/ cranberry stain, $30.00.

Late Paneled Grape, #154

This pattern was produced in crystal, crystal with gold staining, and crystal with color staining. Indiana manufactured this pattern for about ten years from 1913 and continuing in production until about 1923. This pattern was manufactured as a water set, berry set, and a breakfast set. Good quality items can be difficult to find. Indiana may have had some difficulty with the staining process at this time. Most items I have seen have a good deal of fading to the color stain and the gold staining has been fairly worn. There are no known reproductions of this pattern.

Item	Crystal
Bowl, berry/salad, 3-toed, 4.25" d	$15
Bowl, berry/salad, 4.75" d	$15
Bowl, berry/salad, 3-toed, 5.5" d	$18
Bowl, berry/salad, 3-toed, 6.5" d	$28
Bowl, berry/salad, 3-toed, 7.5" d	$44
Bowl, berry/salad, 9" d	$22
Bowl, celery, oblong, 10.5" l	$26
Bowl, pickle, oblong, 8.5" l	$26
Butter w/cover	$59
Celery Vase	$59
Compote, jelly, open, 4.5" d	$32
Compote w/cover, 5.5" d	$89
Creamer	$44
Goblet	$67
Pitcher	$81
Spooner	$37
Sugar w/cover	$59
Tumbler	$37

Late Paneled Grape, tumbler, crystal w/ multicolored stain, $37.00.

Laurel Wreath, #1010

This pattern was manufactured from about 1948 through the mid-1950s and was initially produced in crystal. Two items within this pattern were consistently kept in production. These were the 10" bowl (pictured here) and the 5-part relish (pictured here). The crystal versions of these items went in production from the 1960s through the late 1980s. The milk white versions were made during the late 1950s through the mid-1960s and the olive green versions were produced throughout the 1970s and the early 1980s. The basket and marmalade jar were reintroduced though Tiara Exclusives in 1988 in opalescent pink and again in 1990 in opalescent crystal. These opalescent items were probably not manufactured in Dunkirk. The milk white items, which are the 10.5" bowl ($12), the cake stand ($28), and the 5-part relish ($15) are relatively easy to find.

Item	Crystal
Basket, handled, 12" h	$18
Bowl, berry/salad, 9" d	$15
Bowl, berry/salad, 10" d	$15
Bowl, berry/salad, 10.5" d	$15
Bowl, mayonnaise, 1-handled, 5.5" d	$22
Bowl, mayonnaise, 1-handled, divided, 5.5" d	$22
Bowl, serving, oval, 10" l	$26
Cake Stand, footed, 10" d	$35
Candlestick, low, 1-lite, pr.	$22
Candlestick, 2-lite, pr.	$35
Candlestick, vase, pr.	$30
Candy box w/cover, 7.5" d	$28
Candy box w/cover, 2-part	$28
Comport, 8.5" d	$15
Comport, 9" d	$15
Comport, 10" d	$18
Comport, 10.5" d	$18
Comport, 11" d	$20
Comport, 13" d	$20
Creamer	$15
Cup, punch	$6
Goblet, 8 oz.	$12
Marmalade Jar w/cover	$38
Pitcher, martini	$25
Plate, salad, 7.25" d	$18
Plate, salad, 8" d	$18
Plate, buffet, 14" d	$14
Plate, buffet, 17" d	$14
Relish, 5-part, 14" d	$15
Salver, 14" d	$16
Salver, 13.5" d	$16
Sugar	$15
Tray, creamer/sugar, handled, 8" l	$15
Tumbler, 12 oz.	$10

Laurel Wreath, round 5-part relish platter, olive green, $12.00.

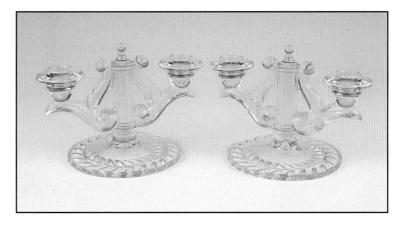

Laurel Wreath, pair of candlesticks, crystal, $35.00.

Laurel Wreath, large serving bowl, milk white, $12.00.

Laurel Wreath, handled footed punch cup, crystal, $6.00.

Leaf, #1009

The exact period of production for this pattern is a little sketchy. However, it can be narrowed down to the late 1940s through the early 1950s. It was probably manufactured for only a few years, as original items in this pattern are very difficult to find. It does appear in some of the older Indiana Glass catalogs; however, dates for the catalogs are uncertain. We do know for sure that the original production was manufactured only in crystal. A few of the pieces, including the tall comport, the low two-lite candlestick, and the lily bowl were reissued during the late 1950s and early 1960s in milk white. During the 1970s several items, including the tall compote (pictured here), the vase candlestick (pictured here) the 8" vase, and the low double candlestick, were made in sunset, black, and sage mist and sold through Tiara Exclusives. In addition, a handled basket, which was not part of the original line, was produced for Tiara. One can easily distinguish between the old and new items simply by the colors.

Item	Crystal	Sunset	Milk White
Candlestick, vase, pr.	$18	$26	-
Candy Box w/cover	$28	-	-
Comport, tall, 6" d	$22	$32	$18
Comport, low, 7.25" d	$20	-	-
Comport, low, 9" d	$25	-	-
Comport, low, 10" d	$25	-	-
Comport, low, 10.5" d	$25	-	-
Comport, low, 11" d	$30	-	-
Comport, low, 13" d	$30	-	-
Cup, punch, footed	$8	-	-
Plate, buffet, 17" d	$26	-	-
Punch set, 15-piece	$240	-	-
Salver, 13.5" d	$28	-	-
Salver, 14" d	$28	-	-
Vase, 8" h	$16	-	-

Item	Crystal	Sunset	Milk White
Bowl, berry, cupped, 10.5" d	$32	-	-
Bowl, center, low	$45	-	-
Bowl, lily, 8.5" d	$38	$64	$26
Bowl, mayonnaise w/ladle	$35	-	-
Candlestick, low, 1-lite, pr.	$25	-	-
Candlestick, low, 2-lite, pr.	$35	-	$22
Candlestick, tall, 2-lite, pr.	$46	-	-

Leaf, candleholder, sunset, $26.00.

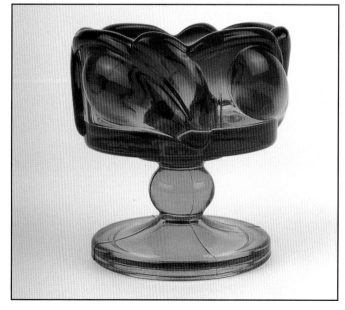

Leaf, tall open compote, sunset, $32.00.

Lily Pons, #605

This pattern dates back to at least 1934 and was originally produced in crystal and green. Production of this pattern had stopped by the late 1930s. In the late 1950s Indiana began reissuing the 7" berry bowl. This bowl remained in continuous production until the 1990s, being offered in crystal ($8), amber ($13), iridescent gold ($18), milk white ($12), olive green ($12), pink decorated ($33), blue decorated ($23), ruby red decorated ($15), and teal ($18). The 2-handled celery was also reissued and remained in continuous production into the early 1980s and was offered in crystal ($10), amber ($10), iridescent gold ($18), olive green ($12), and teal ($15). It is quite probable that these two items were produced in more colors than I have listed. You may be able to use a black light test to distinguish old crystal items from the new crystal items.

Item	Crystal	Green
Bowl, berry/salad, 7" d	$10	$26
Bowl, mint, 6" d	$15	$32
Bowl, celery, 2-handled, 8" l	$10	$34
Bowl, celery, 4-handled, 8" l	$25	$64
Creamer	$15	$24
Cup, fruit or sherbet	$8	$16
Bowl, pickle, no handles, 8" l	$22	$36
Plate, dinner, 9.25" d	$34	$44
Plate, luncheon, 8.5" d	$14	$28
Plate, sherbet, 6" d	$15	$25
Preserve, 7" d	$8	$22
Sugar, handled	$15	$24

Lily Pons, pair of luncheon plates, crystal, $28.00.

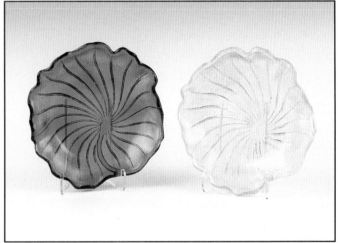

Lily Pons, pair of mint plates, teal & crystal, $12.00 & $15.00.

Lily Pons, creamer & sugar, green, $48.00.

Lily Pons, set of handled relish bowls, crystal, green, & amber, $10.00, $34.00, & $10.00.

Lily Pons, pair of berry/salad bowls, crystal & olive green, $10.00 & $12.00.

Loganberry, #606

There are only three items that appear to exist for this pattern. I have not seen any other items in the older catalogs and this is all I have been able to find for sale on the market. Originally produced in crystal and green, the 7" mint bowl continued in production well into the late 1980s and was manufactured in amber ($10), crystal ($12), iridescent gold ($18), milk white ($12), olive green ($12), and ruby red decorated ($15). This pattern is also sometimes referred to as *Mulberry*, and can be easily confused with other similar patterns made by Imperial, Fenton, and others.

Item	Crystal	Green
Bowl, mint, 7" d	$12	$20
Plate, grill	$10	$22
Plate, salad	$10	$20

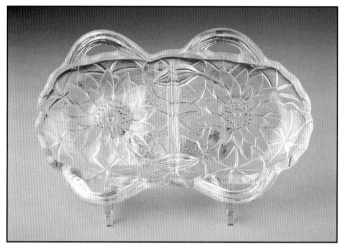

Lily Pons, four-handled oblong relish, crystal, $25.00.

Loganberry, pair of mint bowls, iridescent gold & frosty mint, $17.00 & $12.00.

Lily Pons, set of sherbets, crystal, $32.00.

Loganberry, grill plate, crystal, $10.00.

Loop and Jewel

This National Glass Company pattern was in full production by 1904 and continued in production until about 1907. Items for this pattern are fairly well documented and can be found in numerous reference books. You may find this pattern referred to as *Jewel and Festoon* and/or *Venus*. There are no known reproductions of this pattern.

Item	Crystal
Bowl, berry/salad, 6" d	$21
Bowl, berry/salad, 7" d	$44
Bowl, berry/salad, 8" d	$35
Bowl, mint, square, 5"	$23
Bowl, pickle, oval, 8" l	$21
Bowl, sauce, flat, 4" d	$15
Bowl, sauce, flat, 4.5" d	$15
Bowl, sauce, footed, 4" d	$15
Bowl, sauce, footed, 4.5" d	$15
Butter w/cover	$78
Compote, open, low, 6.5" d	$88
Creamer, berry, footed	$45
Creamer, flat	$45
Cup, punch or custard	$22
Goblet	$40
Pitcher, water, 64 oz.	$98
Plate, mint, square, 5.25"	$23
Salt, master	$52
Shaker	$67
Spooner	$37
Sugar w/cover, footed	$60
Sugar, berry, footed	$40
Syrup	$78
Tumbler	$37
Vase	$57
Wine	$43

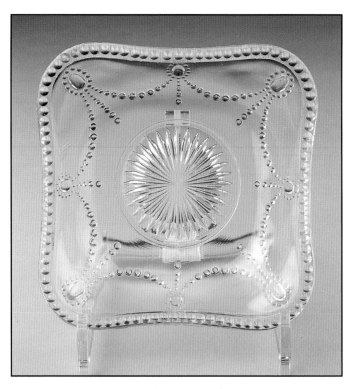

Loop & Jewel, square mint plate, crystal, $23.00.

Lorain, #615

Indiana Glass Company began production of this beautiful pattern in 1929. The floral basket design pattern is part of a very art deco shape. Produced for only three short years in crystal, green, and yellow, manufacturing of this pattern ended in 1932. There are no known reproductions of this pattern.

Item	Crystal	Green	Yellow
Bowl, cereal, 6" d	$54	$270	$200
Bowl, berry/salad, 7.25" d	$116	$54	$78
Bowl, berry/salad, 8" d	$205	$135	$200
Relish, 4-part, 8" d	$33	$33	$43
Bowl, serving, oval, 9.75" l	$65	$65	$81
Creamer, footed	$22	$32	$32
Cup	$33	$33	$26
Plate, sherbet, 5.5" d	$11	$24	$31
Plate, salad, 7.75" d	$16	$20	$25
Plate, luncheon, 8.5" d	$50	$32	$60
Plate, dinner, 10.25" d	$65	$130	$100
Platter, 11.5" l	$34	$66	$82
Saucer	$6	$18	$14
Sherbet, footed	$33	$48	$42
Snack tray, crystal trim	$55	-	-
Sugar, footed	$22	$32	$32
Tumbler, footed, 9 oz.	$33	$36	$50

Loop & Jewel, tri-handled footed sugar, crystal, $45.00.

Lorain, creamer & sugar, yellow, $64.00.

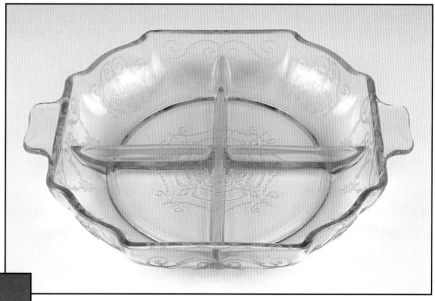

Lorain, handled 4-part
relish, green, $33.00.

Lorain, open candy,
milk white, $10.00.

Lotus Blossom, #1007

This is one of those patterns that began its life in the late 1940s. While initially produced in crystal, crystal etched, and crystal with ruby staining, there were several items that were also made in crystal with amber staining. This pattern was primarily designed as a service set and breakfast set with an expanded compliment of console or decorator items, most notably, baskets and candlesticks. What most collectors find today is the 6" comport (pictured here). This comport remained in continuous production from the early 1960s through the late 1980s and was manufactured in a variety of colors including amber, chartreuse stained, crystal, milk white, olive green, orange stained, violet stained, ice blue, etched blue, and etched green. A few of the items, which includes the sugar and creamer (pictured here) and several of the bowls were produced in milk white during the late 1950s and early 1960s.

Item	Crystal w/ Ruby
Basket, handled, 12" h	$45
Bowl w/ladle, mayonnaise, 5" d	$26
Bowl, berry/salad, 8.5" d	$15
Bowl, berry/salad, 9.5" d	$15
Bowl, berry/salad, 9.75" d	$15
Bowl, berry/salad, 10.5" d	$25
Bowl, berry/salad, 12.5" d	$25
Bowl, nappy, handled, 5.5" d	$12
Candlestick, 1-lite, pr.	$35
Candlestick, deluxe, 2-lite, pr.	$62
Candlestick, vase, deep, pr.	$50
Candlestick, vase, flared, pr.	$50
Candy Box w/cover, footed, 3-part, 6.5"	$42
Candy Box w/cover, footed, 6.5"	$42
Cigarette Box w/cover	$26
Comport, 6" d	$15
Comport, 7" d	$15
Comport, 9" d	$20
Comport, 10" d	$20
Comport, 10.5" d	$20
Comport, 11" d	$25
Comport, 13" d	$25
Creamer, handled	$22
Cup, punch	$10
Marmalade Jar w/cover	$38
Mint Dish, footed	$28
Plate, buffet, 14"	$18
Plate, buffet, 17"	$22
Plate, serving, 11"	$18
Puff Box w/cover	$45
Relish, 3-part, 7" d	$18
Relish, 7" d	$18
Relish, oval, 12" l	$20
Relish, oval, 3-part, 12" l	$20
Salver, 14" d	$18
Sugar, handled	$22
Tray, for creamer/sugar, oval, 8" l	$18
Tray, oval, 2-part, 8" l	$18
Vase, flared, 8" h	$32
Vase, straight, 8" h	$32

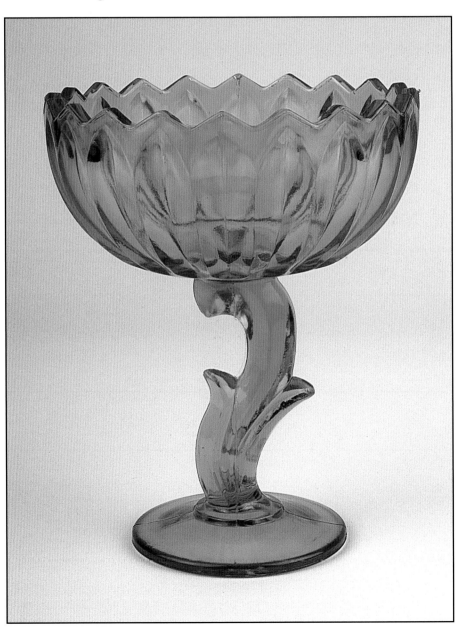

Lotus Blossom, open compote, blue, $20.00.

Lotus Blossom, creamer & sugar, milk white, $20.00.

Lotus Blossom, oval relish, crystal w/ ruby stain, $18.00.

Lotus Blossom, single candlestick, crystal, $17.00.

Lotus Blossom, footed candy box w/ cover, crystal w/ ruby stain, $42.00.

Moderne Classic, #602, #603

What many have referred to in the past as *Moderne Classic* was really a blend of several pattern lines and decorations. Indiana decorated the blank patterns of #602, #603, and #607. However, most folks buying and selling this style item simply refer to all decorated items as *Moderne Classic*. Patterns #602 and #603 are essentially the same. Both were plain paneled patterns, however, #603 had two vertical ribs separating each panel. This pattern was very similar to Indiana's *Artura* pattern #608. If you like art deco, you will like this pattern. This pattern was introduced circa 1930 and was manufactured into the early 1940s. There are no known reproductions of this pattern.

Item	Decorated
Bowl, berry/salad, handled, 8.5" d	$26
Bowl, console, rolled edge, 12" d	$35
Bowl, console, footed, 9.75" d	$18
Bowl, console, footed, deep, 9.25" d	$22
Bowl, center/fruit, footed, 12" d	$32
Bowl, nappy, handled, 6" d	$15
Bowl, preserve, deep, 5.5" d	$20
Bowl, preserve, shallow, 6.5" d	$22
Candlestick, pr.	$38
Cheese Stand, 6"	$25
Plate, handled, 7" d	$15
Plate, no handles, 7" d	$15
Plate, handled, 10" d	$22
Plate, no handles, 10" d	$22
Server, sandwich, center handled, 10.5" d	$28

Moderne Classic, candlestick, yellow & white w/ platinum stain, $16.00.

Moderne Classic, console bowl, yellow & white w/ platinum stain, $18.00.

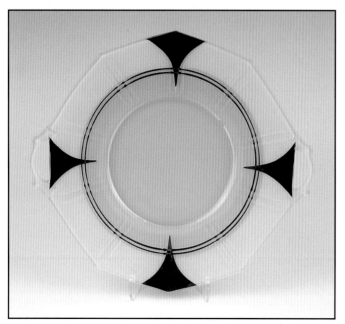

Moderne Classic, handled cake/serving tray, yellow & white w/ platinum stain, $22.00.

Monticello

This pattern made its debut in 1966 with production limited to crystal. By the mid-1970s, many of the items in this pattern were being manufactured in milk white, sunset, blue, etched blue, lime green, and etched green. In the early 1980s, the rose bowl (pictured here) was produced in yellow mist and distributed through Tiara Exclusives. The pattern itself is often confused with Imperial's *Mt. Vernon* pattern. There are no known reproductions of this pattern.

Item	Crystal	Milk White
Basket, handled, 8.75" h	$24	$18
Bowl, nappy, 6" d	$18	$12
Bowl, oval, 8.75" l	$15	$10
Bowl, relish, rectangular, 12" l	$15	$10
Bowl, relish, square, 7" w	$18	$12
Bowl, rose, 6" d	$18	$12
Candlestick, 2-lite, pr., 4" h	$25	$20
Candy Box w/cover, 6" d	$26	$18
Comport, 7.5" d	$25	$16
Comport, 10.5" d	$22	$12
Comport, 12.5" d	$22	$12
Creamer	$18	$15
Sugar w/cover	$22	$18
Vase, handled, 7" h	$25	$18
Vase, swung	$20	

Monticello, nut/rose bowl, yellow mist, $22.00.

Monticello, serving platter, crystal, $22.00.

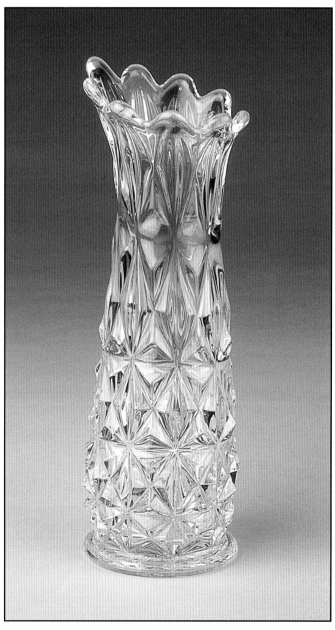

Monticello, swung vase, crystal, $20.00.

Mt. Vernon

It seems every glass company had a *Mt. Vernon* pattern and Indiana Glass was no exception. *Mt. Vernon* began production in 1968 with full production ending about 1987. This pattern was produced as a salad set and beverage set, with a few accoutrements, and was manufactured in amber, smoky blue, crystal, and olive green. The smoky blue was only made for a year or two upon its initial introduction and is very hard to find.

The high-footed candy box and the candle lamp continued in production until the late 1980s. While the candy box continued to be manufactured in its original colors of crystal, amber, and olive green, the candle lamp was manufactured in light blue, light blue etched, pink, pink etched, crystal etched, decorated ruby red, light green, and light green etched. These candle lamps are becoming collectible in a market of their own and their values range from $10 - $20. There are no known reproductions of this pattern.

Mt. Vernon, candy box w/ cover, crystal, $12.00.

Item	Crystal	Olive Green	Amber
Bowl, master salad, 10" d	$10	$14	$12
Bowl, individual salad, 5" d	$4	$6	$5
Candle Lamp	$10	$18	$15
Candy Box, low, round, w/acorn finial on cover, 5"	$12	$18	$15
Candy Box, high, footed, w/cover	$12	$18	$15
Goblet, iced tea, 12 oz.	$5	$10	$8
Goblet, water, 9 oz.	$5	$10	$8
Goblet, juice, 4 oz.	$5	$8	$6
Sherbet, 4.5 oz.	$4	$6	$5

Mt. Vernon, salad set, olive green, $38.00.

Mt. Vernon, candy boxes w/ covers, crystal & olive green, $12.00 & $18.00.

Narcissus Spray, #162

This is another floral pattern that was introduced circa 1917. All items in this pattern were produced in crystal, crystal with gold stain, and crystal with green and purple stain. Production of this pattern continued until about 1928. This pattern sells very well and collectors continue to seek pieces that have very well preserved colored stain. There are no known reproductions of this pattern.

Item	Crystal
Bowl, berry/salad, 4.25" d	$15
Bowl, berry/salad, 4.75" d	$30
Bowl, berry/salad, 8.5" d	$22
Bowl, berry/salad, 9.5" d	$32
Bowl, celery, oval, 10.5" l	$35
Bowl, nappy, handled, 5.5" d	$20
Bowl, pickle, oval, 8.25" l	$25
Bowl, relish, oval, 5.25" l	$15
Butter w/cover	$69
Celery, handled	$37
Compote, jelly, 4.5"	$30
Creamer	$37
Goblet	$33
Pitcher, 64 oz.	$98
Plate, cake or serving	$37
Spooner	$30
Sugar w/cover	$44
Tumbler	$27
Wine	$22

Mt. Vernon, water goblet, olive green, $10.00.

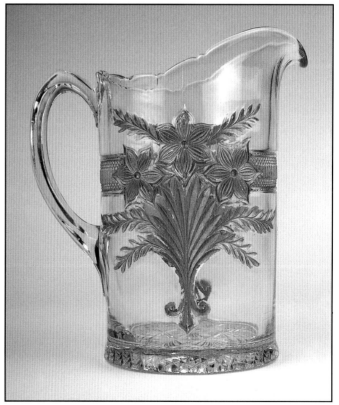

Narcissus Spray, water pitcher, crystal w/ gold stain, $98.00.

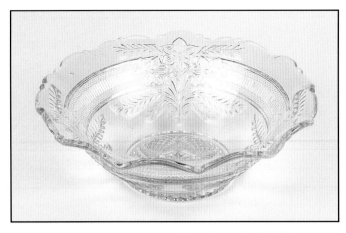

Narcissus Spray, master berry/salad bowl, crystal, $32.00.

Nogi

This pattern began production circa 1906 and was manufactured until about 1915 in crystal and crystal with gold staining. Collectors today also refer to this pattern as *Pendant* or *Amulet*. This pattern is very similar to several other starred designs with oval patterns. To distinguish this pattern from other similar patterns look for the twin threaded ribs separating the clear oval panels. All footed items such as the creamer, sugar, and pitcher have an octagonal foot. There are no known reproductions of this pattern.

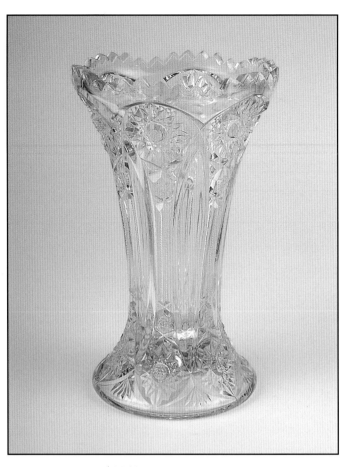

Nogi, vase, crystal, $25.00.

Item	Crystal
Bowl, berry/salad, 5.5" d	$25
Bowl, berry/salad, crimped, 6.5" d	$30
Bowl, berry/salad, 8.5" d	$45
Bowl, celery, oval, 8.5" l	$25
Bowl, console, low, 10" d	$25
Bowl, nappy, square, 4.25" w	$15
Bowl, pickle, leaf-shaped	$15
Bowl, sauce, 4.75" d	$15
Butter w/cover	$52
Compote, 6"	$74
Creamer	$37
Creamer, berry	$37
Goblet	$35
Pitcher, milk	$69
Pitcher, water	$69
Spooner	$30
Sugar w/cover	$44
Sugar, berry	$29
Tray, fan-shape	$23
Tumbler	$27
Vase, 6.5"	$30
Vase, 8"	$25

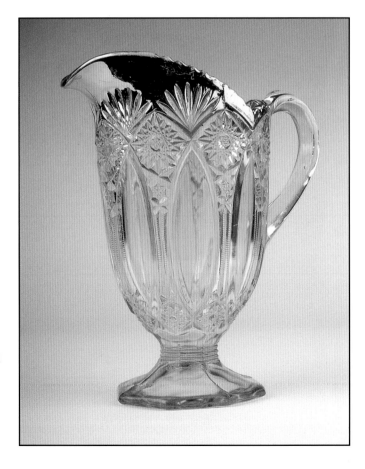

Nogi, milk pitcher, crystal w/ gold stain, $75.00.

Old English, #172

This simple ringed pattern was manufactured by Indiana Glass from 1926 to 1929. It was manufactured in green, amber, pink, crystal, and decorated crystal. To distinguish this threaded pattern from others, look for several bulbous ribs in addition to the fine ribs. These bulbous ribs will be at the bottom of the footed pieces and towards the center of the flat pieces. This pattern is relatively easy to find in green but the other colors can be a challenge. Keep in mind that all the covered items have the cloverleaf shape handle on the lid. All handled items have a distinctive ear-shaped handle setting them apart from the norm. There are no known reproductions of this pattern.

Old English, pair of footed tumblers, amber, $60.00.

Item	Crystal	Green	Pink	Amber
Bowl, flat, 4" d	$19	$30	$24	$24
Bowl, footed, fruit, 9" d	$21	$46	$43	$43
Bowl, flat, 9.5" d	$26	$42	$38	$38
Candlesticks, pair, 4" h	$26	$45	$43	$43
Candy Dish, w/cover, flat	$42	$70	$65	$65
Compote, 2-handle, 6.5" d	$12	$30	$25	$25
Compote, 7" d	$12	$32	$27	$27
Compote, 3.5" d	$12	$27	$22	$22
Creamer	$10	$22	$19	$19
Egg Cup	$10	-	-	-
Fruit Stand, footed, 11" d	$19	$58	$49	$49
Goblet, 8 oz.	$16	$42	$38	$38
Pitcher	$36	$90	$81	$81
Pitcher, w/cover	$57	$160	$146	$146
Plate, w/indent	$10	$28	$22	$22
Sandwich server, center handle	-	$70	$62	$62
Sherbet, 2-styles	$10	$26	$22	$22
Sugar w/cover	$15	$65	$57	$57
Tumbler, 4.5" footed	$12	$38	$30	$30
Tumbler, 5.5" footed	$18	$46	$43	$43
Vase, fan type, 5.5" h	$25	$75	$70	$70
Vase, footed, 8" h	$21	$67	$59	$59
Vase, footed, 8.25" h	$21	$67	$59	$59
Vase, footed, 12" h	$33	$90	$81	$81

Old English, pair of egg cups, crystal, $20.00.

Old English, fruit stand, green, $58.00.

Oval Star, #300

This is one of the few patterns that Indiana manufactured as a child's toy service. This pattern was manufactured circa 1910 and made only in crystal. This pattern has a twenty-pointed star in an oval panel and there are no known reproductions.

Item	Crystal
Butter w/cover	$46
Creamer	$33
Pitcher	$46
Spooner	$26
Sugar w/cover	$39
Tumbler	$23

Oval Star, toy creamer & sugar, crystal, $72.00.

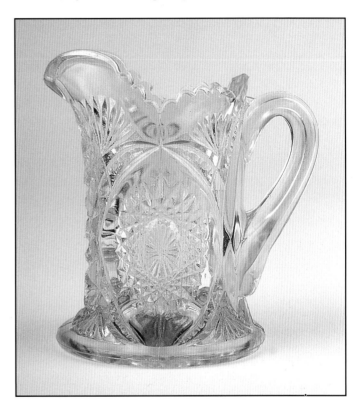

Oval Star, toy water pitcher, crystal, $46.00.

Oval Star, toy tumblers, crystal, $115.00.

Paneled Daisy and Finecut, #123

Introduced as early as 1905, this pattern was made for both the commercial and consumer markets. However, it had a much greater impact in the consumer market. Often confused with other similar patterns, such as Imperial's *Octagon*, this pattern can be distinguished by three vertical panels of stars or daisies separated by an oval field of finecut. The name can be somewhat misleading as the stars are not daisies in the traditional sense (i.e. Daisy and Button). There were quite a variety of items made in the pattern and the more recent issues are relatively easy to find. Original crystal pieces are a little harder to locate, but are still available at reasonable prices. The sunset and iridescent amethyst colors were manufactured during the 1970s and Indiana reissued this pattern in black from 1975 through 1979.

Paneled Daisy & Finecut, round master berry/salad bowl, crystal, $44.00.

Item	Crystal	Sunset	Amethyst	Black
Basket, handled, 9.5" h	-	$45	-	-
Basket, handled, footed, 9" h	-	$50	$50	-
Bowl, berry/salad, 8.5" d	$44	$50	-	$35
Bowl, berry/salad, crimped, 10" d	$52	$50	-	-
Bowl, berry/salad, crimped, flared, 9" d	$44	-	-	-
Bowl, berry/salad, 4.75" d	$22	$20	-	$10
Bowl, cabarette, 11" d	$40	-	-	-
Bowl, nappy, 4"	d	$25	-	-
Bowl, orange, flat	$58	-	-	-
Bowl, pickle, oval, 8" d	$23	-	-	-
Bowl, relish, oval, 4.5" l	$18	-	-	-
Bowl, rose, 6.5" d	-	$35	-	-
Butter w/cover	$75	$45	$55	$36
Cake Stand, 14" d	$75	$150	-	-
Candle Holder/Punch Stand	$20	$35	$45	-
Celery Vase	$59	-	-	-
Compote w/cover, high, 6.5" d	$88	-	-	-
Compote, jelly, open	$37	-	-	-
Creamer	$44	$25	$25	$20
Cruet w/stopper, 7 oz.	$63	-	-	-
Cup, punch or custard	$22	$10	$13	-
Goblet, 8 oz.	$40	$20	$25	$15
Pitcher, 32 oz.	$100	$50	$70	-
Pitcher, 54 oz.	$140	$50	$60	$35
Plate, buffet, 14" d	-	$45	-	-
Plate, dessert, 5.5" d	$15	$20	-	-
Plate, cake or serving, 12" d	$52	$30	-	-
Punch Set, 11 pcs.,	$170	$200	$275	-
Sugar	$59	$25	$25	$20
Tumbler, 9 oz.	$37	$20	-	-
Vase, swung, 11" h	-	$35	$45	-
Wine	$37	-	-	-

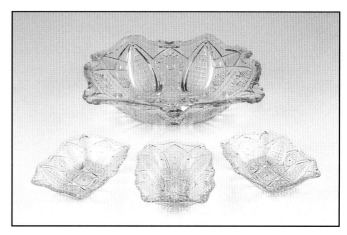

Paneled Daisy & Finecut, rectangular berry/salad bowl set, crystal, $35.00.

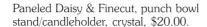

Paneled Daisy & Finecut, punch bowl stand/candleholder, crystal, $20.00.

Paneled Daisy & Finecut, cruet (w/o stopper), $25.00.

Paneled Heather, #126

Introduced circa 1911, this pattern was produced in crystal, crystal with gold staining, and crystal with green and purple staining. It is difficult to near impossible to find items with the gold staining one hundred percent intact. However, many of the items still have the colored staining in very good condition. Many folks get this confused with Bryce's *Paneled Daisy* or *Paneled Forget-me-not*. On this pattern, *every* other panel has plant stalks with several small flowers. There are no known reproductions of this pattern.

Item	Crystal
Bowl, berry/salad, 4-toed, 4.25" d	$15
Bowl, berry/salad, 5.5" d	$22
Bowl, berry/salad, 6.5" d	$25
Bowl, berry/salad, 7" d	$28
Bowl, berry/salad, 7.5" d	$44
Bowl, berry/salad, 8.5" d	$46
Bowl, berry/salad, crimped, 8" d	$46
Bowl, berry/salad, crimped, 9" d	$48
Bowl, berry/salad, oval, 4-toed, 6.5" l	$29
Bowl, nappy, 4.25" w	$15
Bowl, relish, oval, 8.5" l	$15
Bowl, sauce, oval, 6.5" l	$15
Bowl, sauce, round, 4.75" d	$18
Butter w/cover	$63
Cake Stand, 10.5" d	$74
Celery Vase	$59

Item	Crystal
Compote w/cover, 6.5" d	$52
Compote w/cover, jelly, 4.5" d	$46
Creamer, berry	$44
Creamer, large	$44
Cruet, 8 oz.	$52
Goblet	$40
Pitcher, 64 oz.	$86
Sherbet	$10
Spooner	$39
Sugar w/cover, large	$59
Sugar, berry, open	$37
Tumbler, 8 oz.	$37
Vase, 6.5" h	$44
Wine	$37

Paneled Heather, bowl, crystal, $44.00.

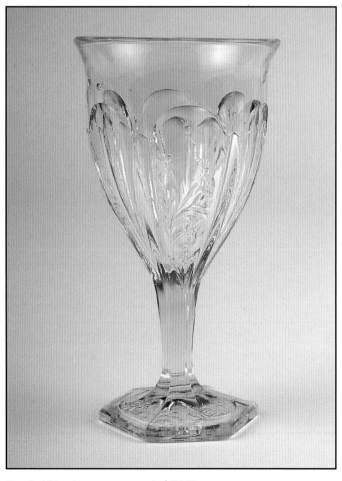

Paneled Heather, wine, crystal, $37.00.

Paneled Heather, butter w/
cover, crystal w/ multicolored
stain, $75.00.

Paneled Heather, footed
sherbet, crystal, $10.00.

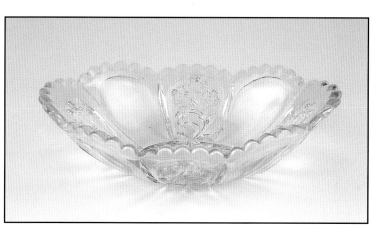

Paneled Heather, oval
sauce bowl, crystal, $15.00.

Paneled Strawberry, #127

Introduced circa 1911, this pattern was produced in crystal, crystal with gold staining, and crystal with green and red staining. This pattern is easily distinguishable with several panels of large strawberries lying overtop a Greek key band which wraps around the middle. Look for the Greek key band to distinguish it from other strawberry style patterns. There are no known reproductions of this pattern.

Item	Crystal
Bowl, berry/salad, 4.75"	$23
Bowl, berry/salad, 8.5"	$69
Butter w/cover	$100
Celery Vase	$59
Creamer	$58
Goblet	$80
Pitcher, 64 oz.	$120
Spooner	$58
Sugar w/cover	$90
Tumbler	$37

Paneled Strawberry, tumbler, crystal w/ multicolored stain, $45.00.

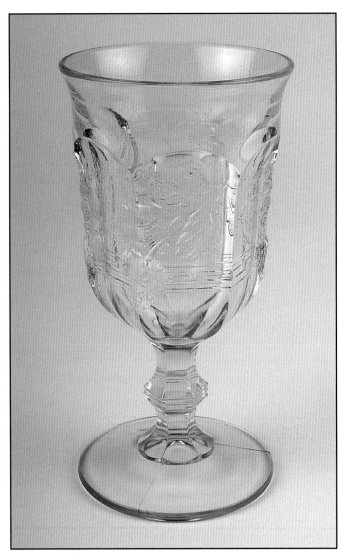

Paneled Strawberry, water goblet, crystal, $80.00.

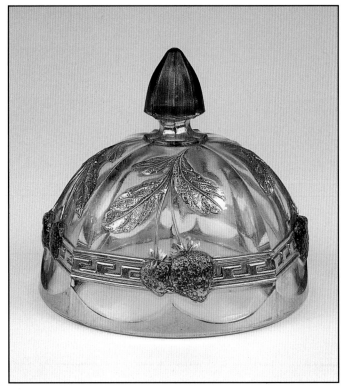

Paneled Strawberry, butter cover, crystal w/ multicolored stain, $50.00.

Park Lane

This pattern appears to have begun as a Colony Glass product and was shifted over to Dunkirk for production. Most likely designed to imitate Imperial's *Cape Cod* pattern, *Park Lane* was introduced around 1965 and was first produced solely in crystal. Its popularity was such that Indiana Glass began manufacturing this pattern in olive green and amber by 1968. In 1976, Indiana had a limited production run of this pattern in blue. This line was available only as a beverage set and luncheon set. There are no known reproductions of this pattern.

Item	Crystal	Blue	Green	Amber
Cocktail, 4 oz.	$4	$6	$5	$4
Cordial, 1.5 oz.	$4	$8	$6	$4
Goblet, water, 7 oz.	$4	$6	$5	$4
Plate, salad, 8" d	$8	$12	$10	$6
Sherbet, 7 oz.	$4	$6	$5	$4
Tumbler, iced tea, 11.5 oz.	$8	$12	$10	$6
Tumbler, juice, 5.5 oz.	$10	$14	$12	$8
Wine, 4.5 oz.	$4	$8	$6	$5

Park Lane, set of wines, olive, $24.00.

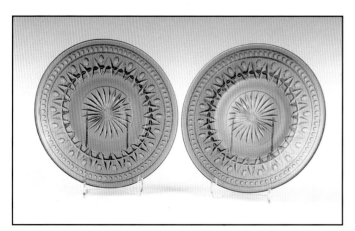

Park Lane, pair of salad plates, blue, $24.00.

Pebble Leaf, #6

This pattern was initially introduced in the 1930s in crystal and green. It was introduced again in the 1950s in crystal with a light blue edging. It was reissued again in 1982 in crystal. The punch bowl has been in continuous production from the 1950s through the 1980s. During the 1960s, the punch bowl was manufactured in milk white and sold under the name of *Orleans*. By far, the 13" egg hors d'oeuvres tray is what you will find for sale out in the market. That item was produced consistently from the 1950s through the 1980s in various colors including amber ($18), crystal ($16), iridescent blue ($37), and olive green ($16).

Item	Crystal	Green
Bowl, dessert, 4" d	$5	$15
Bowl, jelly, handled, 7"	$21	$36
Bowl, nappy, handled, 4.5" d	$10	$20
Bowl, olive, handled, 5.25"	$10	$20
Bowl, relish, 2-part, 8.25"	$12	$18
Bowl, relish, 2-part, 10.5"	$12	$18
Bowl, relish, 3-part, 10"	$12	$18
Bowl, salad, handled, 8" d	$6	$15
Candleholder, pr.	$12	-
Cup, punch	$5	-
Egg Hors d'oeuvres, 13"	$16	-
Goblet, juice, 6 oz.	$14	-
Goblet, water, 12 oz.	$10	-
Plate, bread, 5.5"	$8	$18
Plate, cheese, 6"	$8	$18
Plate, dessert, 4.5"	$8	$18
Plate, dinner, 10.5"	$12	$20
Plate, salad, 8.25"	$12	$20
Punch Bowl, 12.5 qt.	$55	-
Punch Bowl, 5 qt.	$46	-
Punch Bowl, 9.5 qt.	$55	-
Salt/Pepper, pr.	$15	-
Tidbit, 2-tier	$22	-
Tumbler, iced tea, 15 oz.	$12	-
Tumbler, rocks, 9 oz.	$12	-

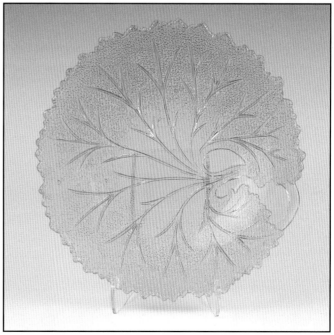

Pebble Leaf, dinner plate, green, $20.00.

Pebble Leaf, water goblets, crystal &
crystal w/ ruby stain, $10.00 & $15.00.

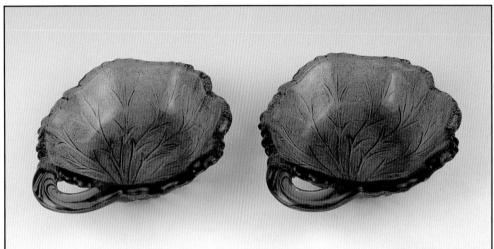

Pebble Leaf, pair of handled
nappies, amber, $10.00.

Pebble Leaf, handled divided
relish, crystal, $10.00.

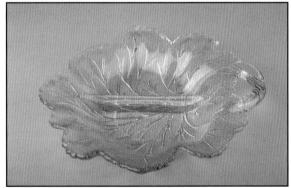

Pebble Leaf, pair of handled
dessert plates, crystal, $16.00.

Pineapple and Floral, #618

The initial period for the production of this pattern was from 1932 to 1937 and it was manufactured only in crystal. As the market changed, many pieces of this pattern were reissued in a variety of colors, including fired on red (1950s), amber (1960s), avocado green (1960s), milk white (1950s, 1970s), pink (1980s), cobalt blue (1980s), and fired on light blue (1950s). Probably the most reissued pieces of this pattern were the diamond-shaped comport and the 7" bowl. These two items were reissued on and off in crystal well into the 1990s. If you want to collect a full set, your best bet is to collect the crystal. Full sets were not manufactured in all colors.

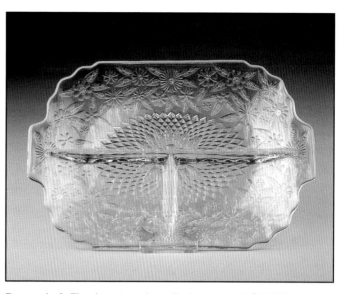

Pineapple & Floral, rectangular grill plate, crystal, $15.00.

Item	Crystal	Amber	Fired on Red
Ashtray, 4.5" l	$19	$22	$22
Bowl, berry/salad, 4.5" d	$27	$25	$23
Bowl, berry/salad, 7" d	$5	$25	$11
Bowl, cereal, 6" d	$32	$27	$27
Bowl, cream soup	$24	$24	$24
Bowl, serving, oval, 10" l	$31	$33	$33
Comport, diamond-shaped	$5	$10	$10
Creamer, diamond-shaped	$10	$11	$11
Cup	$11	$11	$11
Plate, dinner, 9.5" d	$16	$18	$18
Plate, salad, 8.5" d	$10	$12	$12
Plate, sandwich, 11.5" d	$22	$25	$25
Plate, sherbet, 6" d	$7	$8	$8
Plate, w/indentation, 11.5" d	$27	-	-
Platter, closed-handle, 12" l	$19	$21	$21
Platter, relish, divided, 11.5" l	$21	$25	$25
Saucer	$6	$8	$8
Sherbet, footed	$21	$25	$25
Sugar, diamond-shaped	$10	$11	$11
Tumbler, 8 oz.	$42	$42	$42
Tumbler, 12 oz.	$54	$50	$50
Vase, cone-shaped	$65	$47	$47

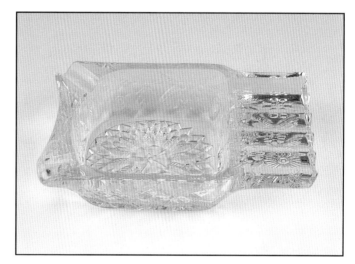

Pineapple & Floral, ashtray, crystal, $19.00.

Pineapple & Floral, diamond-shaped compote, crystal, $5.00.

Pineapple & Floral, berry/salad bowl, crystal, $5.00.

Ponderosa Pine

This was a late pattern issued strictly through Tiara Exclusives and manufactured in crystal, chantilly green, etched crystal, and spearmint. The crystal items, which are widely available, were produced from 1981 through 1998. Chantilly green items were produced for only two years from 1986 to 1987, but items are available and a full set can still be assembled. Harder to find are the items produced in etched crystal and spearmint. Etched crystal was produced for one year only in 1994 and spearmint (a slightly darker green than the chantilly green) was produced for one year only in 1998.

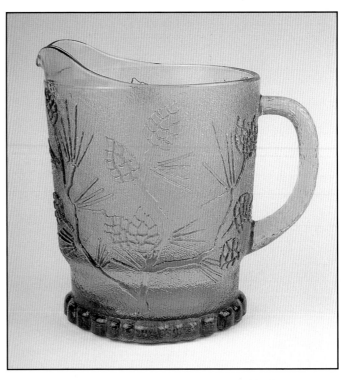

Ponderosa Pine, water pitcher, spearmint green, $35.00.

Item	Crystal	Chantilly Green
Bowl, berry/salad, 5" d	$10	15
Bowl, berry/salad, 9.5" d	$18	$22
Bowl, serving or vegetable, 7.75" d	$12	$16
Bowl, soup	$9	$15
Goblet, 12 oz.	$8	$12
Mug, handled, 13 oz.	$12	$14
Mug, handled, 9 oz.	$8	$10
Pitcher, 74 oz.	$24	$35
Plate, dinner, 10" d	$14	$16
Plate, salad, 8" d	$10	$12
Plate, serving, 12.5" d	$15	$16
Plate, tidbit, handled, 10" d	$16	$20
Salt/Pepper, pair	$18	$22
Tray, egg, 12.5" d	$15	$16
Tray, relish, 3-part, 12.5" d	$15	$16
Tumbler, 18 oz.	$10	$12
Tumbler, juice, 9 oz.	$8	$10

Ponderosa Pine, salad set, crystal, $48.00.

Ponderosa Pine, serving tray, chantilly green, $16.00.

Ponderosa Pine, pair of shakers, crystal, $18.00.

Pretzel, #622

This pattern was initially issued in crystal in the mid-to late 1930s. Because this pattern was machine made, Indiana produced it in large quantities. This is evident by how much is out in the collectible market seventy years later. Production of this pattern continued into the early 1940s. To add a twist Indiana began producing this pattern with a fruit intaglio in the center. These items are in slightly more demand and you may wind up paying a couple extra dollars for them.

During the 1950s, Indiana used the small berry bowl for promotional purposes and as a result you may find some items with transfers in the center advertising a particular product. They also produced some in the same terrace green color that they used for the *Christmas Candy* pattern.

Indiana decided to use this pattern in the early 1970s to create an astrological series, which was sold through Tiara Exclusives and was produced in a variety of colors, including amber and olive green.

Last but not least, the oval celery has had the longest history. It was produced on and off for over fifty years, its last production date being in the late 1980s. Indiana produced the oval celery in amber ($8), crystal ($12), iridescent gold ($10), milk white ($15), and olive green ($8).

Item	Crystal
Bowl, berry/salad, 4.5" d	$8
Bowl, berry/salad, 9.5" d	$19
Bowl, celery, oval, 10.25" l	$12
Bowl, nappy, handled, 6" l	$7
Bowl, olive, leaf-shape, 7" l	$12
Bowl, pickle, handled, 8.5" l	$6
Bowl, soup, 7.5" d	$11
Creamer, footed	$10
Cup	$8
Pitcher, 39 oz.	$540
Plate, dessert, 6" d	$3
Plate, dinner, 9.5" d	$11
Plate, salad, 8.5" d	$6
Plate, sandwich/cake, 11.5" d	$19
Plate, snack w/indent, square, 7.25" w	$10
Plate, square, 7.25" w	$10
Saucer	$3
Sugar, footed	$10
Tumbler, iced tea, 12 oz.	$73
Tumbler, juice, 5 oz.	$52
Tumbler, water, 9 oz.	$57

Pretzel, sandwich/cake plate, crystal w/ intaglio, $19.00.

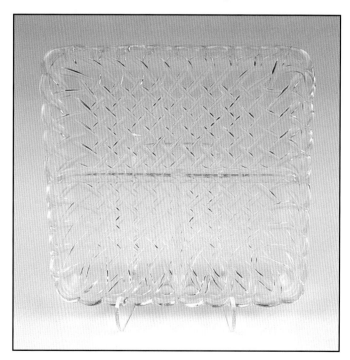

Pretzel, square divided plate, crystal, $10.00.

Pretzel, pair of soup bowls, crystal, $11.00.

Pretzel, pair of oblong celery bowls, amber & olive green, $8.00 & $8.00.

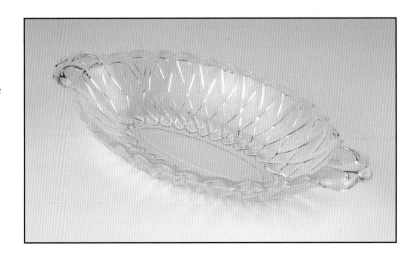

Pretzel, creamer & sugar, crystal, $20.00.

Pretzel, oval handled pickle bowl, crystal, $6.00.

Pyramid, #610

The Pyramid pattern was manufactured as an entertainment set with thirteen pieces. Plates, cups, and saucers were never produced. The pattern was produced from 1926 to 1932 and was manufactured in crystal, green, pink, and yellow. The 4-part relish, the berry bowls, and the tumbler were reissued through Tiara Exclusives. The 4-part relish was reissued in both blue and black colors. They are valued at $25 each. The large and small berry bowls, along with the 8-ounce tumbler, were reissued only in black. They are valued at $25, $15, and $25, respectively.

Item	Crystal	Green	Pink	Yellow
Bowl, berry/salad, 4.75" d	$22	$38	$38	$59
Bowl, berry/salad, 8.5" d	$32	$68	$59	$81
Bowl, oval, 9.5" l	$32	$49	$70	$43
Bowl, pickle, handled, 9.5" l	$32	$38	$38	$68
Creamer	$22	$36	$38	$43
Ice Tub, w/lid	$103	$151	$161	$243
Pitcher	$427	$286	$427	$594
Relish Tray, 4-part, handle	$27	$70	$65	$73
Sugar	$19	$36	$38	$43
Tray for creamer and sugar	$27	$32	$32	$59
Tumbler, footed, 11 oz.	$81	$92	$70	$103
Tumbler, footed, 2 styles, 8 oz.	$59	$59	$59	$81

Pyramid, pair of berry/salad bowls, black, $30.00.

Pyramid, handled 4-part relish, blue, $25.00.

Rayed Flower, #132

This pattern was introduced circa 1905 and was produced in crystal and decorated crystal until about 1920. Called *Splendor* by many collectors, one can easily identify this pattern by the six pointed star within the six flower-shaped petals with the entire flower having rays extending outward. There is also diagonal starred banding around the top of the pattern. There are no known reproductions of this pattern.

Item	Crystal
Bowl, berry/salad, 3-toed, 4.5" d	$14
Bowl, berry/salad, 3-toed, 7.5"	$44
Bowl, berry/salad, oval, 4-toed, 9.5"	$40
Bowl, mint, 3-toed, 5.5" d	$15
Bowl, nappy, handled, 5.5" d	$15
Bowl, nappy, heart-shaped, 6.5" d	$23
Bowl, pickle, oval	$17
Butter w/cover	$59
Cake Stand, 9.25"	$65
Celery Vase	$59
Compote w/cover, 6.5" d	$89
Creamer	$44
Cup, custard or punch	$22
Honey Dish w/cover	$120
Pitcher, milk	$82
Pitcher, water, 64 oz.	$82
Shaker	$66
Spooner	$37
Sugar w/cover, handled	$59
Toothpick Holder	$52
Tumbler	$37
Wine	$28

Rayed Flower, covered compote (w/o cover), crystal, $35.00.

Rayed Flower, tumbler, crystal, $37.00.

Rayed Flower, punch cup, crystal, $22.00.

Rayed Flower, set of footed berry/salad bowls, crystal, $42.00.

Recollection

Federal Glass initially manufactured this pattern as *Madrid* during the Depression Era. Then in 1976, Federal Glass recreated the molds (because the molds had been scrapped during WWII) and reissued this pattern. Federal Glass distinguished the re-issuance of this pattern by adding a "76" in the design and by only making it in an amber color. When Federal Glass closed in 1978, Indiana Glass bought the molds, removed the "76" and reproduced the pattern again.

The initial reproduction of this pattern by Indiana was made in crystal. It was later reproduced in light blue, pink, and teal. In most cases, it is easy to tell the difference between Federals' initial production of this pattern in the 1930s and Indiana's reproduction of this pattern in the 1980s, simply because the original molds were of a much higher quality. The newer pieces are much heavier and the detail just is not there. In addition, Indiana's blue is brighter than the original and Indiana's pink is much lighter than that of Federal.

Indiana created several new items for this pattern that were not offered by Federal Glass, by combining the candlestick with other items. For example, the cake plate was created by gluing the 10" plate onto the candlestick, the hurricane lamp/vase was created by gluing the 15 oz. tumbler onto the candlestick, the footed candy dish was made by gluing the butter dish onto the candlestick, and the center bowl was created by gluing the 9.5" bowl to the candlestick. Acknowledging Indiana's production of this pattern as a contribution to the advancement of the glassware industry is up for debate. However, Indiana's 100 years of success was the result of them reinventing what had already existed.

Recollection, goblet, blue, $22.00.

Item	Crystal	Blue	Pink	Teal
Bowl, berry/salad, 6.75" d	$4	$14	$6	$16
Bowl, berry/salad, 9.5" d	$10	$17	$15	$25
Bowl, serving, oval, 10" l	$15	$28	$20	$32
Butter w/cover	$17	$36	$26	$48
Cake Stand, 10.25" d	$28	$58	$46	$65
Candleholder, pair	$12	$28	$14	$35
Candy Dish w/cover, pedestal	$15	$24	$20	$38
Compote, open, 9.5" d	$26	$37	$41	$64
Creamer, 3.25"	$8	$15	$12	$18
Cup	$4	$9	$8	$12
Goblet, 12 oz.	$10	$22	$18	$28
Plate, dinner, 10.25" d	$10	$16	$14	$20
Plate, grill, 10.25" d	$17	$25	$22	$36
Plate, relish, 2-part, 10.25" d	$17	$25	$22	$36
Plate, salad, 7.5" d	$4	$12	$9	$15
Salt/Pepper	$20	$30	$27	$35
Saucer	$4	$9	$8	$12
Sugar	$8	$15	$12	$18
Tumbler, 11 oz.	$7	$16	$15	$20
Tumbler, 15 oz.	$10	$18	$16	$25
Vase, 8.25"	$10	$18	$15	$20

Recollection, butter w/ cover, blue, $36.00.

Recollection, open compote, crystal, $26.00.

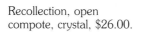

Recollection, serving bowl, crystal, $10.00.

Recollection, dinner plate with cup & saucer, crystal, $26.00.

Rose Point Band, #153

This pattern was first introduced in 1913 in crystal and goofus. Some of the other names describing this pattern may be more appropriate, such as *Water Lily* and *Clematis*, but we will stay with convention. This pattern is unique in that the design is not deep. The pressing is shallow, giving it a more "etched" look and feel, rather than the heavy patterns that were typical of Indiana. Production of this pattern was definitely finished by 1918 and I suspect it ended much earlier. All the items I have found are very well pressed and the detail is not mottled as happens when molds are used extensively. There are no known reproductions of this pattern.

Items	Crystal
Bowl, berry/salad, 4.5" d	$15
Bowl, berry/salad, 7.5" d	$25
Bowl, berry/salad, footed, 8" d	$28
Bowl, berry/salad, flared, 9" d	$35
Bowl, berry/salad, oval, 9.5" l	$42
Bowl, berry/salad, crimped, 10" d	$44
Bowl, sauce, flat	$15
Bowl, sauce, footed	$29
Butter w/cover	$60
Cake Stand, 9" d	$59
Cake Stand, 10" d	$74
Celery Vase	$59
Compote w/cover, 5.5" d	$59
Compote w/cover, 6.5" d	$74
Compote w/cover, 7.5" d	$89
Compote, jelly, open	$37
Creamer, berry, 4-toed	$44
Creamer, large, flat	$44
Cruet w/stopper	$54
Goblet	$37
Pitcher, water, 62 oz.	$82
Spooner	$37
Sugar w/cover, berry, 4-toed	$37
Sugar w/cover, large, flat	$59
Tumbler	$37
Wine	$37

Rose Point Band, butter w/ cover, crystal, $60.00.

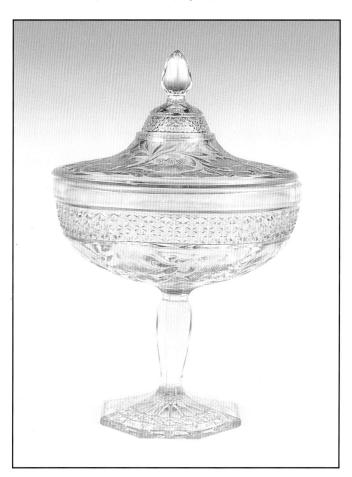

Rose Point Band, compote w/ cover, crystal, $89.00.

Rose Point Band, footed creamer, crystal, $44.00.

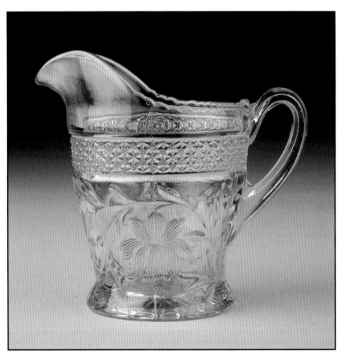

Rose Point Band, flat creamer, crystal, $44.00.

Rosette with Pinwheels, #171

There were not too many patterns produced that were similar to this one, making this pattern rather unique. Production for this pattern began in the late 1920s and is known to exist only in crystal. You can distinguish this pattern by noting the eight-petal rosette with flowers on the end of each petal. The sugar, spooner, creamer, and pitcher are all cone-shaped, giving the pattern an art deco flair. The pattern appears to have finished production by 1932. There are no known reproductions of this pattern.

Item	Crystal
Bowl, berry/salad, 3-toed, 5.5" d	$25
Bowl, berry/salad, 4-toed, 9.25" d	$38
Bowl, pickle, oval, handled, 7" l	$25
Butter w/cover	$65
Cake Stand, 9.5" d	$50
Compote w/cover, jelly, 4.75" d	$45
Compote w/cover, 6.25" d	$62
Creamer	$32
Cup, custard or punch, footed	$10
Honey Dish w/cover	$84
Pitcher, 64 oz.	$78
Spooner	$16
Sugar w/cover	$36
Tumbler	$20
Wine	$15

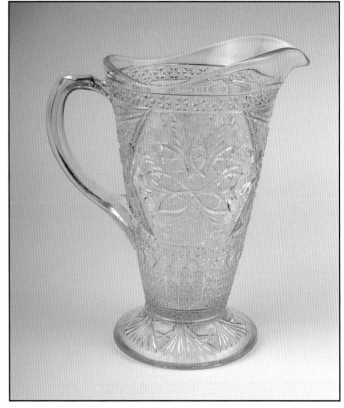

Rosette with Pinwheels, water pitcher, crystal, $78.00.

Rosette with Pinwheels,
creamer & spooner,
crystal, $32.00 & $16.00.

Rosette with Pinwheels, footed individual
berry/salad bowl, crystal, $25.00.

Shooting Star, #119

This little known pattern was made as early as 1904
and manufactured only in crystal. Production appears
to have ended for this pattern by 1908. This pattern was
limited to a berry set and a breakfast set. There are no
known reproductions of this pattern.

Item	Crystal
Bowl, berry/salad, 4"	$15
Bowl, berry/salad, 4.5"	$15
Bowl, berry/salad, 6"	$22
Bowl, berry/salad, 7"	$30
Bowl, olive, oval, 6" l	$15
Butter w/cover	$52
Creamer	$37
Spooner	$38
Sugar w/cover	$45

Shooting Star, butter w/ cover, crystal, $52.00.

Shrine

Possibly one of Beatty-Brady's earliest patterns, *Shrine* is a perfect example of the exquisite craftsmanship and talent that this early company possessed. Referred to by many collectors as *Jeweled Moon and Star*, this pattern was produced circa 1896 and remained in production until 1905. Easily identifiable by the crescent moons and five point stars on the stippled background of every other panel. The clarity of the glass is very good with several of the items demanding a fairly high price. The artistry involved with this pattern is quite exquisite and continues to satisfy many collectors. There are no known reproductions of this pattern.

Item	Crystal
Bowl, berry/salad, 6.5"	$36
Bowl, berry/salad, 7.5"	$45
Bowl, berry/salad, 8.5"	$52
Bowl, berry/salad, 9.5"	$58
Bowl, pickle, oval	$60
Bowl, relish, oval	$40
Bowl, rose	$75
Bowl, sauce, 4"	$22
Butter w/cover	$100
Cake Stand, 8.5" d	$140
Celery Vase	$80
Compote w/cover, 6.5" d	$82
Compote, jelly	$44
Creamer	$66
Goblet	$92
Mug	$69
Pitcher, milk, 32 oz.	$110
Pitcher, water, 64 oz.	$340
Platter	$92
Shaker	$89
Spooner	$67
Sugar w/cover	$90
Toothpick Holder	$160
Tumbler	$60

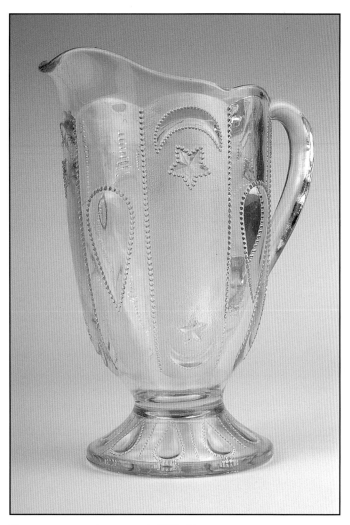

Shrine, water pitcher, crystal, $350.00.

Shrine, jelly compote, crystal, $44.00.

Spanish American

There are two versions of this pattern, which collectors fondly call *Dewey* and *Gridley*. *Gridley* is believed to be an original Beatty-Brady pattern, while *Dewey* is thought to be a transfer from the Indiana Tumbler and Goblet Company. The *Dewey* pattern revolves around cannonballs while the *Gridley* pattern revolves around mortar shells. *Dewey* is relatively easy to find, however you will have to look a little harder for the *Gridley* pitcher. While both pitchers could have been produced as early as 1898, the production of the *Dewey* pitcher in Dunkirk would not have occurred until after 1903. All known production of these items is limited to crystal. An unknown company, most likely overseas, has been recently reproducing the *Gridley* pitcher in a wide variety of colors, including the green, which is pictured here.

Item	Crystal
Pitcher (Gridley)	$265
Pitcher (Dewey)	$145
Tumbler (Dewey)	$55

Spanish-American, tumbler, crystal, $55.00.

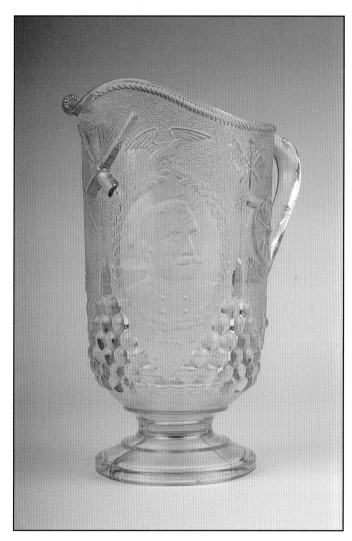

Spanish-American, water pitcher, crystal, $145.00.

Spanish-American, reproduction water pitcher, green, $25.00.

Spiraled Triangle, #106

This is another very detailed pattern from the Beatty-Brady timeframe. Most likely issued in the late 1890s, this pattern was only made until about 1902. Good quality examples are hard to find, making the valuation of most items difficult. The name of this pattern is derived from the series of triangles at the bottom of each item that contains a spiral of beads. The rest of the pattern simply is a confluence of repeating lines similar to many diamond styled patterns of the time. The production of this pattern was limited to a water set, berry set, and breakfast set. There are no known reproductions for this pattern.

Item	Crystal
Bowl, berry/salad, 4.5" d	$15
Bowl, berry/salad, 7.5" d	$20
Bowl, berry/salad, 8.5" d	$25
Bowl, pickle, oval	$25
Butter w/cover	$75
Creamer	$35
Cruet w/stopper	$52
Pitcher	$85
Shaker	$60
Spooner	$35
Sugar w/cover	$35
Tumbler	$24

Spiraled Triangle, oval relish bowl, crystal, $25.00.

Star Band

I run across this pattern quite often. As far as patterns go, it is a fairly nondescript pattern consisting of a single star-in-diamond band at the top of the multi-paneled sides. It was produced in crystal and crystal with gold staining starting circa 1915 and ending around 1931. Also called Bosworth, this pattern can be easily confused with many similar patterns that have plain panels with banding. There are no known reproductions of this pattern.

Item	Crystal
Bowl, berry/salad, 3-toed, 4.25" d	$15
Bowl, berry/salad, 3-toed, 7.5" d	$27
Bowl, berry/salad, 4.25" d	$15
Bowl, berry/salad, 5" d	$17
Bowl, berry/salad, 8.5" d	$30
Bowl, berry/salad, 10" d	$35
Bowl, celery, oval, 10.5" l	$15
Bowl, nappy, handled, 6.5" d	$30
Bowl, pickle, oval, 8.5" l	$16
Butter w/cover	$69
Celery Vase, handled	$37
Compote, jelly, open	$30
Creamer	$37
Cup, punch or custard	$10
Goblet	$33
Pitcher, water, 64 oz.	$81
Spooner	$30
Sugar w/cover	$44
Tumbler	$27
Vase, footed, 6.5" h	$30
Wine	$26

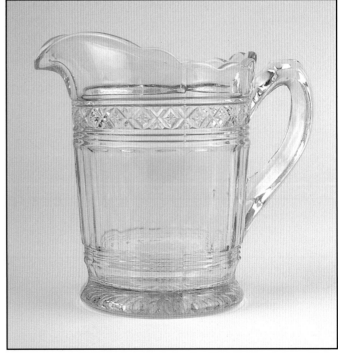

Star Band, creamer, crystal, $37.00.

Star Band, handled nappy, crystal w/ gold stain, $30.00.

Star Band, individual berry/salad bowl, crystal, $17.00.

Star Band, tumbler, crystal, $27.00.

Stippled Sandbur

This is another early Beatty-Brady pattern. Probably introduced circa 1898, it was manufactured until about 1904. This is one of several starred patterns that were popular at the time and as a result has also been referred to as *Stippled Star Variant*. This pattern is most often confused with Gillinder & Sons' *Stippled Star* pattern. To distinguish this pattern from other similar patterns, look for a ten to twelve-point star on a stippled or grained background. Most items in this pattern have a scalloped edge with the color or clarity of the glass having a slight gray tint. There are no known reproductions of this pattern.

Item	Crystal
Bowl, berry/salad	$15
Bowl, berry/salad	$40
Butter w/cover	$52
Celery Vase	$37
Compote, open, jelly	$55
Compote w/cover	$74
Creamer	$37
Goblet	$40
Pickle Jar	$52
Pitcher, water	$81
Spooner	$30
Sugar w/cover	$44
Toothpick Holder	$37
Tumbler	$27
Wine	$22

Stippled Sandbur, jelly compote, crystal, $55.00.

Success

This pattern was introduced circa 1910 and was produced until about 1921. A fairly intricate pattern, it is relatively difficult to find. Segregated from other similar patterns by the notched ribbons which separate the oval field and the starred panels, *Success* can also be distinguished by the raised "X" marks on the handled items such as the bread tray and the cruet (both pictured here). There are no known reproductions of this pattern.

Item	Crystal
Bowl, berry/salad, 5.5" d	$67
Bowl, berry/salad, 8.5" d	$75
Bowl, celery, oval, 10.5" l	$37
Bowl, olive, oval, handled	$37
Bowl, pickle, oval, 8.5" l	$37
Butter w/cover	$150
Celery, vase, handled	$120
Compote, jelly, footed	$150
Creamer, berry	$89
Creamer, large	$89
Cruet w/stopper	$110
Cup, custard or punch	$44
Pitcher, 3-pint	$180
Preserve, handled, footed	$150
Shaker	$130
Spooner	$100
Sugar w/cover, large	$150
Sugar, berry	$60
Tray, bread/cake, handled	$120
Tumbler	$67
Vase, footed	$89

Stippled Sandbur, sugar w/o cover, crystal, $20.00.

Success, handled bread tray, crystal, $120.00.

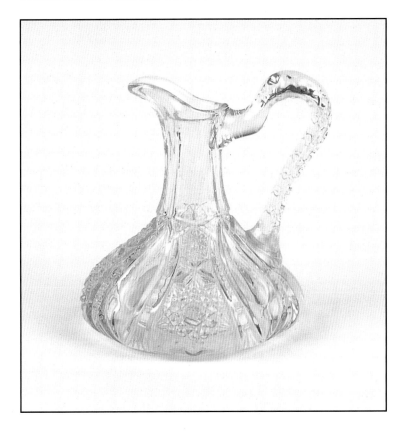

Success, cruet w/o stopper, crystal, $50.00.

Tea Room, #600

This extremely popular pattern appeals to many collectors and continues to be in high demand. Manufactured from 1926 to 1931, and produced mainly in green and pink, this pattern also had limited production in amber and crystal. Green *Tea Room* items are more available than pink, but be careful to inspect all items carefully prior to purchase. This design, with its many edges and corners, is very prone to chipping and bruising. The large crystal vase is easily found. There are two styles of creamers and sugars, a rectangular shape that is not footed and a conical, footed style. This pattern tends to be one of the more expensive depression era patterns that Indiana manufactured. There are no known reproductions of this pattern.

Item	Amber	Crystal	Green	Pink
Bowl, finger	-	$86	$76	$76
Bowl, banana split, flat, 7.5"	-	-	$220	$220
Bowl, banana split, footed	-	$82	$110	$160
Bowl, celery, 8.25"	-	$25	$38	$30
Bowl, salad, 8.75"	-	-	$160	$150
Bowl, oval vegetable, 9.5"	-	-	$82	$72
Candlestick, low, pair	-	-	$88	$94
Creamer, 3.25"	-	-	$34	$32
Creamer, footed, 4.5"	$110	-	$22	$22
Creamer, rectangular	-	-	$28	$22

Item	Amber	Crystal	Green	Pink
Cup	-	-	$72	$65
Goblet, 9 oz.	-	-	$82	$72
Ice Bucket	-	-	$94	$88
Lamp, electric, 9"	-	$150	$190	$160
Marmalade/Mustard, notched lid	-	-	$210	$180
Parfait	-	-	$110	$110
Pitcher, 64 oz.	$650	$440	$190	$170
Plate, sherbet, 6.5"	-	-	$38	$36
Plate, luncheon, 8.25"	-	-	$42	$38
Plate, 2-handled, 10.5"	-	-	$60	$50
Relish, divided	-	-	$34	$28
Salt and Pepper, pair	-	-	$82	$72
Saucer	-	-	$34	$34
Sherbet, low, footed	-	-	$44	$38
Sherbet, low, flared edge	-	-	$34	$28
Sherbet, tall, footed	-	-	$55	$55
Sugar, w/cover, 3"	-	-	$130	$110
Sugar, footed, 4.5"	$110	-	$22	$22
Sugar, w/cover, flat	-	-	$220	$190
Sundae, footed, ruffled edge	-	-	$100	$82
Tray, center-handle	-	-	$220	$170
Tray, rectangular creamer & sugar	-	-	$62	$82
Tumbler, flat, 8 oz.	-	-	$130	$140
Tumbler, footed, 6 oz.	-	-	$38	$38
Tumbler, footed, 8 oz.	$120	-	$38	$38
Tumbler, footed, 11 oz.	-	-	$55	$50
Tumbler, footed, 12 oz.	-	-	$82	$76
Vase, ruffled edge, 6.5"	-	-	$160	$140
Vase, ruffled edge, 9.5"	$375	$55	$190	$160
Vase, straight edge, 9.5"	-	$190	$110	$250
Vase, ruffled edge, 11"	-	-	$380	$430
Vase, straight edge, 11"	-	-	$220	$430

Tearoom, creamer & sugar, pink, $44.00.

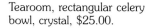

Tearoom, rectangular celery bowl, crystal, $25.00.

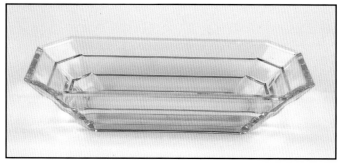

Teardrop, #1011

Introduced in the late 1940s, this pattern was initially produced in crystal and crystal with ruby staining. The footed compotes that we see quite often at flea markets and yard sales were not part of this pattern's original offering. By far the most popular items produced were the large compote (pictured here) and the cake stand (pictured here), which were not original to the pattern. The compote, in varying sizes, was produced in a wide array of colors and remained in production throughout the 1960s, '70s, and '80s. Thanks to the florist industry, these compotes were big sellers. They were produced in milk white ($15), olive green ($15), crystal ($11), amber ($17), etched green ($12), red decorated ($18), pink ($19), etched blue ($22), pewtertone ($12), and probably several more. The cake stand was made in crystal ($27), milk white ($21), amber ($32), and red decorated ($48). Finding original pieces to this pattern is not necessarily an easy feat. There are no known reproductions of this pattern.

Item	Crystal w/Staining
Bowl, berry/salad, 9" d	$12
Bowl, berry/salad, 10.5" d	$16
Bowl, center, footed, 7.5" d	$14
Bowl, mayonnaise, 4.5" d	$10
Bowl, nappy, 2-handled, 7" d	$25
Candlestick, low, 1-lite, 3.25" h, pr.	$55
Candlestick, high, 1-lite, 5" h, pr.	$65
Candlestick, high, 2-lite, 6" h, pr.	$85
Candy Box w/cover, 6" d	$45
Comport, 8.5" d	$30
Comport, 9" d	$30
Comport, 10" d	$30
Comport, 11" d	$35
Comport, 13" d	$35
Creamer	$12
Cup, punch	$4
Plate, mayonnaise, 7.5" d	$15
Plate, 2-handled, 10" d	$23
Plate, sandwich, center handled, 10" d	$45
Plate, buffet, 9" d	$32
Plate, buffet, 14" d	$38
Plate, buffet, 17" d	$38
Salver, 14" d	$45
Salver, 13.5" d	$45
Snack Set	$26
Sugar	$12
Tray, creamer/sugar	$12
Vase, 8"	$26

Teardrop, open compotes, pewtertone, crystal, & red decorated, $12.00, $11.00, & $18.00.

Teardrop, high-footed cake stand, amber, $32.00.

Teardrop, planter, satin green, $8.00.

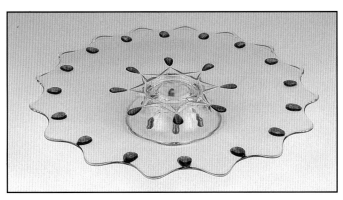

Teardrop, footed serving platter, crystal w/ ruby stain, $45.00.

Twin Feather

This pattern had its beginnings as a Beatty-Brady/National pattern and was made in both crystal and crystal with gold staining. Production for this item started circa 1900 and continued to about 1910. Also known as *Bismarc Star*, this pattern had for many years been misidentified and was stated in several books to exist only in the form of a goblet. Fortunately, we are wiser now and interested collectors can now pursue all twenty-five known items. The quality and clarity of glass for this pattern can vary from piece to piece. There are no known reproductions of this pattern.

Item	Crystal
Bowl, berry/salad, 6" d	$15
Bowl, berry/salad, 7" d	$40
Bowl, berry/salad, 8" d	$55
Bowl, mint, leaf-shaped, 6"	$24
Bowl, mint, square, 5" w	$18
Bowl, celery, oval, 10.5" l	$32
Bowl, console, flared, 10" d	$32
Bowl, nappy, 4.5" d	$15
Bowl, pickle, oval, 8.25" l	$20
Butter w/cover	$69
Compote, jelly, high, 5" d	$30
Compote, low, 6" d	$30
Compote, low, 7" d	$44
Compote, low, 9" d	$75
Creamer	$38
Creamer, berry, footed	$30
Cruet w/stopper	$65
Goblet	$40
Pitcher, milk	$75
Pitcher, water	$98
Spooner	$30
Sugar w/cover	$45
Sugar, berry, footed	$30
Tumbler	$28
Wine	$32

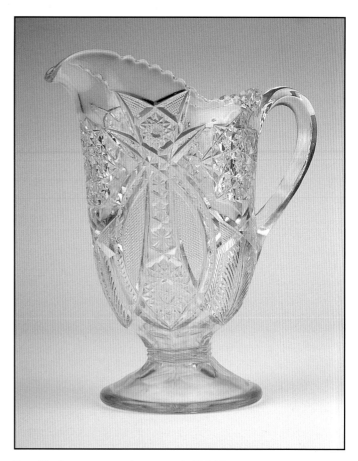

Twin Feather, water pitcher, crystal, $98.00.

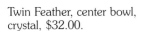

Twin Feather, center bowl, crystal, $32.00.

Twin Feather, set of four wines, crystal, $128.00.

Twin Feather, open compote, crystal, $30.00.

Twin Feather, sugar (w/o cover), crystal, $25.00.

Vernon, #616

Vernon was manufactured for only a few short years from 1930 to 1932. Produced in crystal, green, and yellow, its delicate design has made it a highly sought after pattern as far as depression glass goes. Prices for this pattern are somewhat higher than some of the other Indiana depression glass patterns due to its lack of availability. With some diligent searching, you can find this pattern in crystal. However, it can be much more difficult to gather a complete set in either green or yellow. There are no known reproductions of this pattern.

Item	Crystal	Green	Yellow
Creamer, footed	$14	$34	$34
Cup	$12	$20	$20
Plate, luncheon, 8"	$14	$12	$14
Plate, sandwich, 11.5"	$15	$30	$30
Saucer	$5	$6	$6
Sugar, footed	$14	$32	$32
Tumbler, footed, 5"	$22	$50	$50

Vernon, pair of saucers, crystal, $10.00.

Vernon, pair of lunch plates, crystal, $28.00.

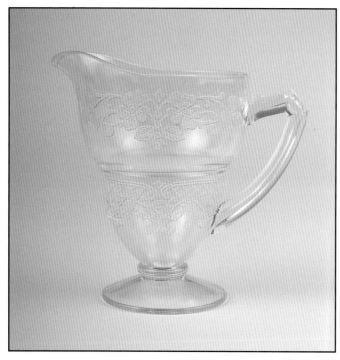

Vernon, creamer, crystal, $14.00.

Vernon, cup, crystal, $12.00.

Village Guild, #1016

Initially issued in the early 1960s as pattern #1016 in crystal and etched crystal, this pattern was reissued in the 1980s and again in the 1990s. A very simple pattern, this line of glass was hand pressed and polished. As a result, the quality is very good. There are no known reproductions of this pattern.

Item	Crystal
Basket, handled, 12"	$35
Bowl, berry/salad, 9"	$18
Bowl, center, 11"	$28
Bowl, mayonnaise, 2-part, 5"	$22
Bowl, mayonnaise, 4"	$22
Bowl, relish, 2-part	$22
Candleholder	$16
Comport, 10.25" d	$28
Comport, 11.5" d	$35
Comport, 13" d	$38
Comport, 14" d	$38
Creamer	$15
Cup, punch	$8
Plate, buffet or serving, 14"	$38
Plate, mayonnaise, 8"	$15
Punch Bowl, footed, 5 qt.	$45
Sugar	$15
Tray, serving, 2-part, 12"	$38

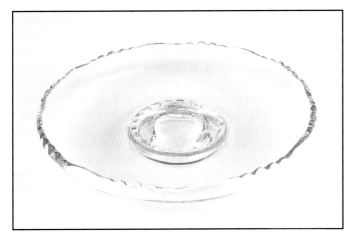

Village Guild, console bowl, crystal, $38.00.

Weavetex, #16

Given the pattern number for this line, this may have been a very early issue. However, my research indicates it was first issued in the 1950s. You could purchase this pattern in a fired-on powder blue color or in crystal. The pattern was manufactured as a berry set and a luncheon set. Bowls are relatively easy to find, especially in the later colors, but plates, cups, and sherbets are very elusive. The later colors include milk white, black, olive green, and iridescent gold which were made throughout the 1960s, '70s, '80s, and '90s. This pattern was promoted as *Basketweave* during the 1960s and the iridescent gold was marketed as *Goldentone* during the 1980s.

Item	Crystal	Green	Gold	Milk White
Bowl, berry/salad, 4"	$5	-	-	-
Bowl, berry/salad, 9"	$12	$10	$15	$12
Cup, fruit	$4	$5	$6	$5
Plate, fruit cup	$9	-	-	-
Plate, luncheon, 6"	$10	-	-	-
Plate, serving, 11"	$15	-	-	-
Saucer	$4	-	-	-
Sherbet	$5	-	-	-

Weavetex, chip & dip set, iridescent gold, $21.00.

Weavetex, serving bowl, olive green, $10.00.

Whirled Sunburst in Circle, #115

This short-lived pattern was manufactured primarily during the National Glass years of Indiana Glass. Made only as a service set, most items are reasonably scarce. Originally a Beatty-Brady pattern, *Whirled Sunburst in Circle* was made up until 1906. This pattern is known to exist only in crystal. There are no known reproductions of this pattern.

Item	Crystal
Bowl, berry/salad, 6" d	$44
Bowl, berry/salad, 7" d	$52
Bowl, berry/salad, square	$42
Bowl, console, flared, 10"	$35
Bowl, nappy, 4" d	$24
Butter w/cover	$82
Creamer	$44
Pitcher, water	$100
Spooner	$38
Sugar w/cover	$59
Tumbler	$38

Whirled Sunburst in Circle, serving bowl, square, crystal, $42.00.

Whirled Sunburst in Circle, center bowl, crystal, $35.00.

Whirled Sunburst in Circle, creamer, crystal, $44.00.

Whitehall, #521

There has been great debate over the years as to the origination of this pattern because the overall design is remarkably similar to Fostoria's *American* pattern. Indiana began producing this pattern after the Lancaster Glass Company purchased Indiana Glass. In order to increase production of popular selling items, many of the molds at Colony Glass were used at the Dunkirk Facility. Colony Glass started producing this pattern in the mid-1950s, but production of this pattern in Dunkirk did not start until 1962. Over the years (1960s - 1980s), this pattern was produced in crystal, olive green, and amber. In the 1990s, this pattern was produced in a light blue, teal blue, and light pink. When Lancaster Colony purchased Fostoria in the mid-1980s, Indiana merged a number of the Fostoria molds into the Whitehall line and renamed the line *American Whitehall*.

To try to reduce the confusion between the Fostoria's *American* pattern and *Whitehall*, there are a couple of things you can look for. First, if the color is anything but crystal, it is *Whitehall*. Fostoria never made any pieces in these colors prior to being purchased by Lancaster. If you are evaluating an item made in crystal, you can give it a black light test, understanding that this is not always practical. Fostoria's glass will glow a pale yellow and Indiana's will not. In addition, you may find a slightly better clarity in Fostoria's glass. If you are evaluating a footed piece, look at the shape of the feet. *American* pieces will have slightly splayed feet, while *Whitehall* will have straight, tapered, octagonal feet. When you are evaluating items such as pitchers and jugs, look at the handles. *American* handles connect right at the top of the pitcher, while the *Whitehall* pattern has handles that attach about an inch or so down from the top. You can also check the bottom of items such as bowls and plates. If the base ring has been ground, then it is a Fostoria product. Indiana ground the bottoms on only a limited number of patterns. This was not one of them. For items such as goblets and tumblers, take a look at the overall shape. *American* pieces will have more of a curve to them with a slight flare at the top. *Whitehall* pieces will be more straight-sided.

Item	Amber	Blue	Crystal	Olive	Pink	Teal
Bowl, mint, 3-toed	-	-	$10	-	$15	$20
Bowl, console/center, 3-toed	-	-	$18	-	$25	-
Bowl, serving, oval	-	-	$13	-	$15	-
Bowl, serving, oval, divided	-	-	$10	-	$12	-
Butter w/cover	-	-	$15	-	$20	-
Candleholder, 2-styles	-	$18	$8	-	$14	-
Candy Box w/cover, 5.5" d	-	$15	$10	-	$12	$16
Creamer	-	-	$8	-	$15	-
Pitcher, 64 oz., two-styles	$20	-	$31	$37	$35	-

Item	Amber	Blue	Crystal	Olive	Pink	Teal
Plate, dinner, 9"	$10	-	$15	$8	-	-
Plate, cake or serving, 3-toed, 12" d.	-	-	$30	-	$32	-
Sherbet, 5 oz.	$3	$4	$5	$5	-	-
Snack Set	$12	-	$20	$18	-	-
Sugar	-	-	$8	-	$15	-
Tidbit, center glass handle	$15	-	$35	$20	-	-
Tumbler, iced tea, 14 oz.	$4	$3	$6	$5	-	$7
Tumbler, juice, 5 oz.	$7	$4	$12	$4	-	$20
Tumbler, water, 10 oz.	$4	$13	$5	$3	-	$6

Whitehall, water pitcher, crystal, $31.00.

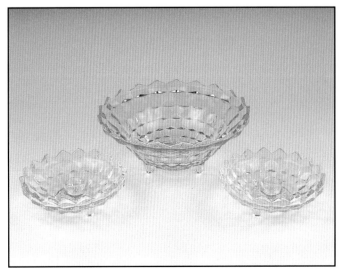

Whitehall, console set, crystal, $34.00.

Whitehall, candy box
w/ cover, teal, $16.00.

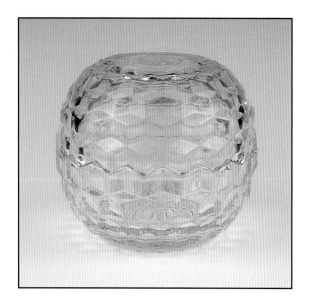

Whitehall, candle
lamp, crystal, $8.00.

Whitehall, oval serving
bowl, crystal, $13.00.

Whitehall, set of four footed
tumblers, amber, $16.00.

Wild Rose, #7

As with the *Weavetex* pattern, the production number for *Wild Rose* is very low, indicating it may have been a very early pattern. I have recently seen a goofus decorated divided relish, which may lend some credence to its early production. The majority of items you will see on the market, however, were produced during the 1950s, '60s, and '70s. Issued as a service set, there are relatively few items associated with this pattern. By far the most predominant items on the market are the milk white and gold iridized berry set. Many folks confuse *Wild Rose* with the *Lily Pons* pattern, especially the *Lily Pons* 7" bowl. There are no known reproductions of this pattern.

Item	Crystal	Irridescent Gold	Milk White
Bowl, berry, 3" d	$5	$8	$4
Bowl, berry, 9" d	$12	$15	$10
Candleholder	$5	$10	$4
Nappy, handled	$5	-	$4
Plate, fruit cup	$5	-	$4
Plate, 2-handled, 10"	$16	-	$12
Relish, handled, 8"	$10	-	$8
Relish, divided, handled, 8"	$10	-	$8

Wild Rose, candleholder, iridescent gold, $10.00.

Wild Rose, handled cake/sandwich plate, crystal, $12.00.

Wild Rose, set of four berry/salad bowls, milk white, $16.00.

Wild Rose, serving bowl, iridescent gold, $15.00.

Wild Rose, handled nappy, crystal, $5.00.

Willow, #1008

I hope that this book will take a lot of the guesswork out of this pattern. Also known as *Oleander* and *Magnolia*, this pattern was made in crystal, crystal with staining, and an emerald green. *Willow* was marketed through various distributors, including Montgomery Wards and Butler Brothers from 1942 through the early 1950s. The creamer and the sugar were made and sold up through 1965. As a result, you will find quite a few of these on the market. You can find many of these items in etched crystal, however, I have seen little to no difference in prices between the crystal and etched crystal items. There are no known reproductions of this pattern.

Item	Crystal w/ Ruby
Basket, handled, 12" h	$45
Bowl, berry/salad, 9.5" d	$15
Bowl, berry/salad, 10.5" d	$25
Bowl, center, oval, 12.5" l	$25
Bowl, console, high-footed, 10.5" d	$34
Bowl, mayonnaise, footed, handled, 5.5" d	$28
Bowl, mayonnaise, footed, handled, divided, 5.5" d	$28
Bowl, rose, 7" d	$32
Candlestick, one-lite, pr.	$35
Candlestick, two-lite, pr., 6" h	$62
Candlestick, vase, pr.	$50
Candy Box w/cover, 6.5" d	$42
Candy Box w/cover, footed, 6.5" d	$42
Comport, 8.5" d	$15
Comport, 9" d	$20
Comport, 10" d	$20
Comport, 10.5" d	$20
Comport, 11" d	$25
Comport, 13" d	$25
Creamer, berry, 6 oz.	$22
Cup, punch, handled	$10
Marmalade Jar w/cover	$38
Plate, buffet, 17" d	$22
Plate, cake, 13" d	$18
Plate, salad, 8" d	$15
Salver, 13.5" d	$18
Salver, 14" d	$18
Sugar, berry, 3" h	$22
Tray, creamer/sugar, 8" l	$18
Tray, relish, 4.25" x 10.75" l	$18
Vase, flared, 10" h	$32

Willow, console bowl, crystal w/ multicolored stain, $25.00.

Willow, console bowl, crystal, $20.00.

Willow, footed candy box w/ cover, crystal w/ ruby stain, $42.00.

Willow, creamer & sugar, crystal, $20.00.

Willow, open compote, milk white, $15.00.

Windsor, Royal Brighton

The Federal Glass Company initially issued the *Windsor* pattern in the early 1970s. Indiana Glass most likely acquired these molds in 1978 at the same time they obtained the molds for the *Recollection* pattern, which Federal also made. Indiana Glass manufactured this pattern from the early 1980s to the mid-1990s and it was produced primarily in crystal, iridescent blue, and pink.

When you go searching for this pattern, you will primarily find the candy bowl with cover and the creamer, sugar, and tray. The candy bowl and cover were made in a variety of colors. The crystal, pink, light blue, and iridescent blue are easily attainable and demand is not that great at the moment. As a result, prices are down. However, Indiana produced the candy bowl and cover in a few harder to find colors. Given the scarcity of those colors, they were probably test runs. If you look hard enough you can find the candy bowl and lid in amber, avocado green, forest green, iridescent teal, peach, ruby red, and teal. All research indicates that Federal manufactured this pattern in crystal only. Therefore, if you own this pattern in crystal, there is no easy way to distinguish Federals production of these items from Indiana's production.

Item	Blue	Crystal	Iridescent Blue	Pink
Bowl, candy, w/cover, 7" d	$17	$15	$25	$17
Bowl, dessert, 5" d	$10	$8	-	$12
Bowl, large, 10.5" d	$18	$12	$36	$28
Bowl, relish, divided, 8.5" d	$18	$12	-	$18
Butter w/cover	-	$18	$28	
Cake Stand, footed	-	$28	-	
Creamer	$10	$8	$16	$10
Marmalade w/cover, 5" h	$18	$12	$32	$18
Mug, handled	$5	$5	-	-
Pitcher, milk	$14	$10	-	-
Plate, bread, 6" d	-	$5	-	
Plate, lunch, 8.5" d	-	$8	-	
Plate, serving, cake, 11" d	$26	$14	-	$26
Salt/Pepper, pair	$18	$18	-	$18
Sugar w/cover, 5" h	$10	$8	$16	$10
Tray, for creamer/sugar, 8.5" l	$10	$8	-	$10
Tumbler, juice, footed, 9 oz.	$8	$5	$10	$8
Tumbler, water, 12 oz.	$8	$5	$13	$8

Windsor, set of three candy bowls w/ covers, blue, crystal, & pink, $17.00, $15.00, & $17.00.

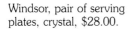

Windsor, pair of serving plates, crystal, $28.00.

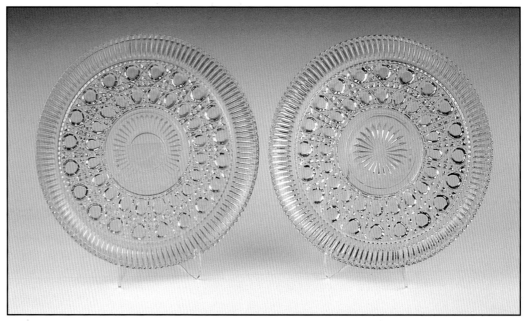

Windsor, creamer & sugar, iridescent blue, $32.00.

Windsor, round handled divided relish, crystal, $12.00.

Windsor, butter w/ cover, crystal, $18.00.

Windsor, creamer, sugar & tray, crystal, $24.00.

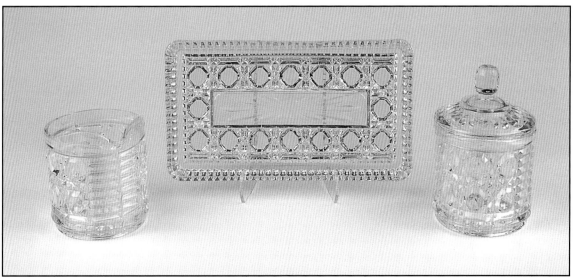

Restaurant, Hotel, and Soda Fountain Glassware

This chapter has been specifically set aside to allow collectors of Indiana Glass a small glimpse of the glassware that was produced for the restaurant, hotel, and soda fountain industry as well as hospitals and other civic industries. With the exception of the items that have been pictured, no market values have been determined. The lack of these documented values should not suggest that these items have no intrinsic value. It simply means that they are not being openly sold or traded and values have not yet been recorded or tracked. Most of these patterns are fairly generic in style, but each pattern maintains a certain beauty and character that the American public has seen continuously evolve over the last century.

Each pattern contains a list of known items that were manufactured. It should not be very difficult to collect an entire set of any of these patterns since many of them were in continuous production for fifty to seventy years.

Number 8

Number 8, cheese dish w/ cover, crystal, $15.00.

Number 9

Number 9, three-part round relish, crystal, $16.00.

Number 12

Ashtray, round, 5" d
Candy Tray, oblong, 8" l

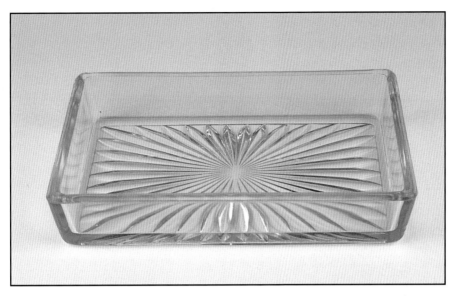

Number 12, rectangular candy tray, crystal, $10.00.

Number 125

Bowl, berry/salad, small
Bowl, berry/salad, medium
Bowl, berry/salad, large
Bowl, relish, oval, flat, 7" l
Bowl, relish, oval, 3-toed
Bowl, relish, handled
Butter w/cover
Celery Vase
Compote, open, jelly
Creamer, berry, 4-toed
Creamer, large
Goblet
Preserve, handled, footed
Shaker
Spooner
Sugar w/cover, large
Sugar, berry, open, 4-toed
Tumbler, 8 oz.
Vase, 6.5" h

Number 125, handled nappy, crystal, $12.00.

Number 125, oval handled
relish, crystal, $10.00.

Number 163

Bowl, berry/salad, 4.25" d
Bowl, berry/salad, 4-toed, 4.25" d
Bowl, berry/salad, 4.75" d
Bowl, berry/salad, 5.5" d
Bowl, berry/salad, oval, 4-toed, 6.5" l
Bowl, berry/salad, belled or crimped, 6.5" d
Bowl, berry/salad, 4-toed, 7.5" d
Bowl, berry/salad, 7.5" d
Bowl, berry/salad, 8.5"
Bowl, berry/salad, belled or crimped, 9"
Bowl, celery, oval, 10.5" l
Bowl, pickle, oval, 8.5" l
Bowl, nappy, square, 4.25" w
Bowl, nappy, square, 8.25" w
Bowl, relish, oval, 6.5"
Butter w/cover
Cake Stand, 8.5" d
Cake Stand, 10.5" d
Celery Vase
Compote w/cover, 4.5" d
Compote w/cover, 5.5" d
Compote w/cover, 6.5" d
Compote w/cover, 7.5" d
Compote, open, jelly, 4.75" d
Compote, open, 6.5" d
Compote, open, 8" d
Compote, open, crimped, 8" d
Creamer, berry
Creamer, large
Cruet, 8 oz.
Cup, custard or punch
Goblet
Pitcher, 48 oz.
Pitcher, 64 oz.
Preserve, handled, footed, 5.5" d
Sherbet, 3.5" d
Spooner
Sugar w/cover, large
Sugar, berry, open
Tumbler, 8 oz.
Vase, 6.5" h
Wine

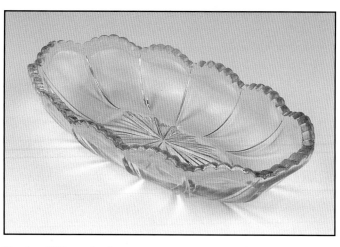

Number 163, oval celery
bowl, crystal, $8.00.

Number 164

Items, Crystal
Bowl, berry/salad, 4.5" d
Bowl, berry/salad, 4.75" d
Bowl, berry/salad, 5.5" d
Bowl, berry/salad, belled, 6.5" d
Bowl, berry/salad, crimped, 6.5" d
Bowl, berry/salad, 7.5" d
Bowl, berry/salad, 8.5" d
Bowl, berry/salad, belled, 9" d
Bowl, berry/salad, crimped, 9" d
Bowl, berry/salad, belled, 10" d
Bowl, berry/salad, crimped, 10" d
Bowl, celery, oval, 10.5" l
Butter w/cover, large
Butter w/cover, small
Compote w/cover, jelly
Creamer
Goblet
Pitcher, 64 oz.
Spooner
Sugar w/cover
Tumbler

Number 164, round serving
bowl, crystal, $22.00.

Number 165

Bowl, berry, individual, 4.25"
Bowl, berry, individual, 4.75"
Bowl, berry, master, 6.5"
Bowl, berry, master, 7.5"
Bowl, berry, master, 8.5"
Bowl, mint, deep, 3-toed, 4.75"
Bowl, mint, shallow, 3-toed, 5.5"
Bowl, jelly
Bowl, jelly, tall, footed, 4.75"
Bowl, olive, 2-handled, 7.5"
Bowl, pickle, oval, 8.5"
Butter w/cover
Celery, tall, 2-handled
Comport, footed, flared top, 4.5"
Comport, footed, 5.5"
Creamer, individual, 1.25 oz.
Creamer, 3.5 oz.
Creamer, 5 oz.
Creamer, berry, footed, 6 oz.
Creamer, 8 oz.
Creamer, 12 oz.
Pin Tray, oval 5.5"
Pitcher, 39 oz.
Pitcher, 55 oz.
Pitcher, 68 oz.
Preserve, footed, 2-handled, 5.5"
Shaker
Sugar, w/cover, ground bottom, 4 oz.
Sugar, 2-handled, w/cover, ground bottom, 4 oz.
Sugar, berry, footed, 6 oz.
Sugar, 2-handled, w/cover, ground bottom, 7 oz.
Sugar, 2-handled, w/cover, ground bottom, 10 oz.
Sugar, w/cover, ground bottom, 11.5 oz.
Sugar, large, 12 oz.
Sugar, large, w/cover
Sundae, tall, footed
Straw Jar, 9.5"
Syrup, nickel top
Tumbler
Water Bottle
Vase, 6.5"

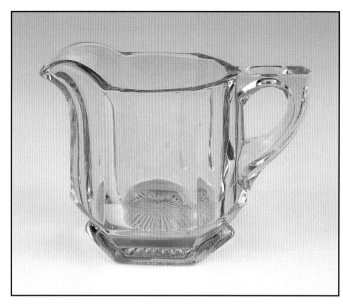

Number 165, berry creamer, crystal, $8.00.

Number 165, open berry sugar, crystal, $8.00.

Number 165, oval celery, crystal, $10.00.

Number 253

Pitcher
Sundae, footed
Tumbler, 6.5 oz.

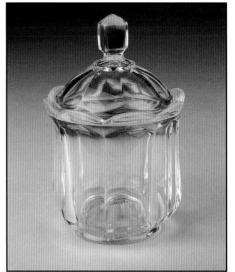

Number 253, sugar w/ cover, crystal, $15.00.

Number 165, large creamer, crystal, $8.00.

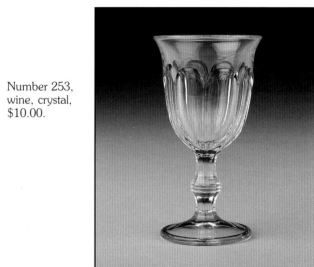

Number 253, wine, crystal, $10.00.

Number 165, small open sugar, crystal, $8.00.

Number 253, round serving bowl, crystal, $15.00.

Number 255

Pitcher
Sundae, footed
Tumbler, 6.5 oz.

Number 258

Banana Split, wide bottom
Banana Split, narrow bottom
Pitcher, w/o ice lip, 72 oz.
Pitcher, w/ice lip, 72 oz
Sundae, footed, crimped
Sundae, clover shaped, footed

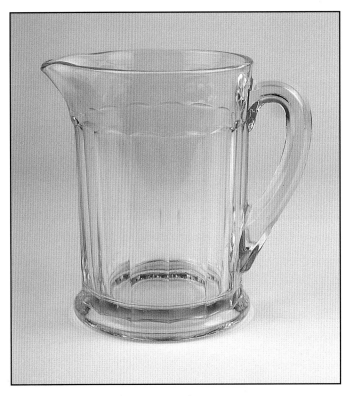

Number 255, water pitcher, crystal, $25.00.

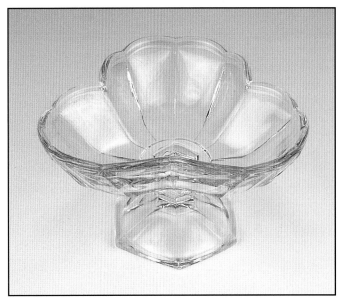

Number 258, footed 3-way sundae, crystal, $22.00.

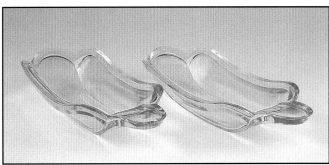

Number 258, pair of banana splits, crystal, $10.00.

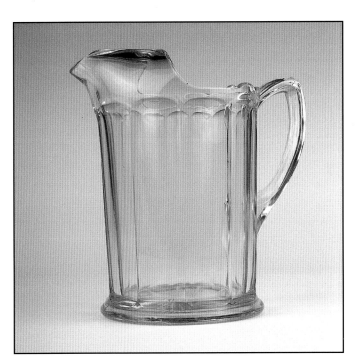

Number 258, water pitcher
w/ ice lip, crystal, $55.00.

Number 304

Banana Split, footed
Bowl, finger
Bowl, relish, 5"
Creamer
Cruet, 4 oz.
Glace
Goblet, water, 9 oz.
Plate, 6"
Plate, 8.5"
Parfait
Salt/Pepper, pair
Sugar, 2-handled
Sundae, low, footed
Sundae, tall, footed
Tumbler, 6 oz.
Tumbler, 8.5 oz.
Tumbler, footed, 6 oz.
Tumbler, footed, 8 oz.
Tumbler, footed, 10 oz.
Tumbler, footed, 12 oz.
Tumbler, footed, 15 oz.

Number 306, footed soda, crystal, $8.00.

Number 306

Tumbler, footed, 12 oz.
Tumbler, footed, 15 oz.

Number 304, set of four footed tumblers, crystal, $100.00.

Number 611

Creamer, berry
Sugar, berry, open
Tray, handled, oval, 8" l
Tumbler, footed, 6 oz.
Tumbler, footed, 8 oz.
Tumbler, footed, 11 oz.
Tumbler, footed, 12 oz.

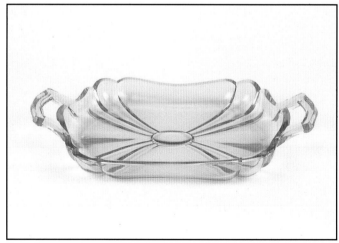

Number 611, handled tray, green, $45.00.

Snack Sets

Daisy and Button

This snack set was manufactured from the mid-1950s through the late 1960s. A full set, which includes four trays and four cups, was produced in crystal ($25), amber ($26), and olive green ($20).

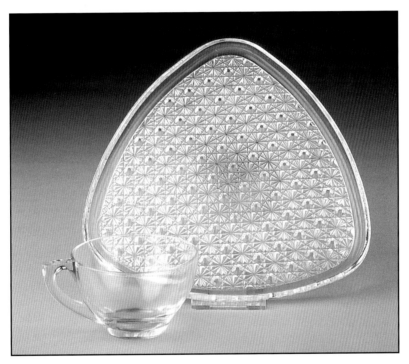

Daisy & Button, snack set, crystal.

Daisy & Button, snack set, olive green.

Snowflake

This snack set was manufactured from the mid-1950s through the late 1960s and was produced only in crystal. A full set, which includes four trays and four cups, is valued at $17.

Snowflake, snack set, crystal.

Sunburst, #625

This snack set began production in the late 1950s and was initially produced only in crystal. From the 1960s through the early 1980s, this snack set was produced in crystal ($10), amber ($12), and olive green ($15).

Sunburst, snack set, crystal.

Miscellaneous

Beaded Edge

This *Beaded Edge* candy box was made from the mid-1960s through the 1980s in a wide assortment of colors including amber ($12), crystal ($8), frosty mint ($15), milk white ($12), satin green ($10), olive green ($10), and wild cherry ($15).

Beaded Edge, covered candy box, footed, olive green, $10.00.

Bicentennial Plates

Glass companies over the years have continually issued special glassware to pay tribute or honor important occasions and persons. Glassware patterns honoring the U.S. centennial, military heroes, presidents, and other important figures in history are always in demand amongst collectors. In keeping with that tradition, in 1976 Indiana Glass issued four patterned plates to celebrate the United States Bicentennial. The plates, inscribed with *Spirit of '76*, *Liberty Bell*, *Independence Hall*, and *American Eagle*, were manufactured in iridescent gold and iridescent blue colors. Presently, values for the iridescent blue plates ($16) are a little higher than the same patterns pressed in iridescent gold ($14). These plates are plentiful and relatively easy to find.

Bicentennial Plate, Spirit of '76, iridescent gold, $14.00.

Bicentennial Plate, Independence Hall, iridescent blue, $16.00.

Bicentennial Plate, Liberty Bell, iridescent blue, $16.00.

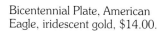

Bicentennial Plate, American Eagle, iridescent gold, $14.00.

Cradle

This unique item was manufactured from the mid-1960s into the early 1970s and was mass-marketed through the florist trade as well as being sold in the department stores of the times. The *Cradle* was manufactured in crystal ($5), golden amber ($8), matte pink ($15), matte blue ($20), milk white ($10), and olive green ($8). This *Cradle* was also made in translucent blue and translucent red, although no value information could be gathered for these colors.

By far, collectors will find that the milk white *Cradle* is the easiest to find as it was made for the longest period of time. Interestingly enough, there are still enough milk glass collectors out there to keep the value above those of amber and olive. The crystal *Cradle* has the lowest value simply through lack of demand.

Cradle, milk white, $10.00.

Fruits

This five-part relish began production in the mid-1970s and continued on and off into the 1990s. There are quite a few of these relish trays on the market right now. One can find it in amber ($15), crystal ($10), olive green ($12), and crystal with staining ($8).

Fruits, 5-part relish platter, amber, $15.00.

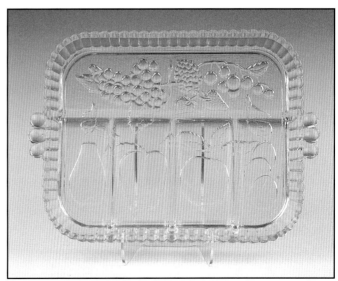

Fruits, 5-part relish platter, crystal, $10.00.

Garland

This tall fruit compote is the only known item in this pattern. *Garland* is the name given to this item by Indiana Glass. Many collectors and novice dealers confuse this pattern with Indiana's #1011 *Teardrop* pattern. While sold directly from Indiana Glass, this compote was also mass-marketed through the florist trade. Indiana manufactured this compote in a variety of colors, including amber ($16), horizon blue ($15), iridescent blue ($18), milk white ($16), olive green ($13), satin blue ($12), and satin green ($10). I am certain that what is included here does encompass all the colors Indiana manufactured this compote in, but interestingly enough I have yet to find this compote in crystal.

Garland, open compote, milk white, $16.00.

Garland, open compote, amber, $16.00.

Glass Days

Held in late spring, this festival started in 1966. Festival attendees can take museum tours, factory tours, etc. These items were given out as souvenirs for attending the festival. Collectors can also find the *Glass Days* promotion imprinted on the Harvest pattern as well as several different styles of ashtrays. Collectors can expect to pay anywhere from $10 to $20 for good quality items.

Glass Days, King's Crown salad plate, crystal w/ cranberry staining, $20.00.

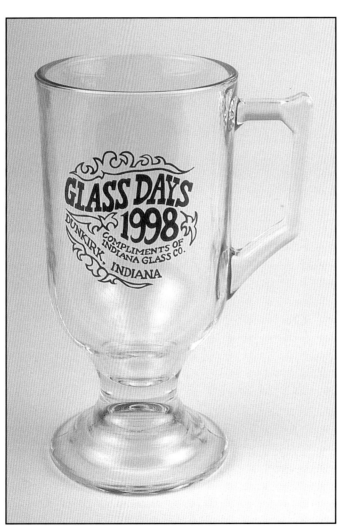

Glass Days, footed mug, crystal, $10.00.

Glass Days, Regency saucer, crystal, $8.00.

Hen On A Nest

The *Hen On A Nest* is probably one of the most prolific glassware items in the history of pressed glassware production. Indiana Glass was just one of many glass factories to produce this product, so it is very important to be able to distinguish between the different hens. Indiana's hen has a closed tail and the head is straight (looking forward). The nest has a beaded edge with striations in the pattern of the nest. These chickens were made from the 1930s through the plant's closure. The hens were manufactured in a variety of colors and collectors can use the color to determine approximate dates of production. Crystal hens ($17) were manufactured continually throughout the history of Indiana Glass. The earlier crystal hens ($20) had their combs painted red. Other earlier colors include yellow ($140) and cobalt blue ($180). Later colors include olive green ($22), milk white ($18), amber ($19), aqua ($30), iridescent blue ($25), iridescent gold ($21), iridescent green ($47), iridescent teal ($41), confederate blue ($50), decorated ruby ($76), decorated cranberry ($95), etched green ($35), horizon blue ($25), teal ($90), pink ($50), and light green ($77). As a notice for all hen collectors, I have recently seen a company purchasing crystal glass hens, flashing color to them, and advertising them for sale on the internet. I see nothing wrong with this as the company is very clear and forthright about what they are doing and the company is placing a sticker on them. Beware, however, of unscrupulous people who may purchase these and try to sell them as old or antiques.

Hen On A Nest, milk white, $18.00.

Hen On A Nest, amber, $19.00.

Honey Dish, #132

I had to include the *Honey Dish* in the book. It is one of those items that is unique to Indiana Glass and has become very collectible over time. This item was produced in crystal as early as 1911 and is easily distinguishable from other patterns with the beehive centered on each side and many bees busily at work.

Collectors will find two types of feet on the *Honey Dish*, those with splayed feet and those with nub feet. I have come across two reasons why Indiana changed the design of the feet. The first reason I found was that the feet had a design flaw and the feet easily cracked or chipped. The second reason I ran across was that Indiana changed in order to move away from the hand pressing of this item, incorporating it in the machine pressed inventory. Whatever the reason, there are two things you as a collector can count on: honey dishes with splayed feet were made before 1971 and honey dishes with splayed feet demand quite a bit more money than the later issues.

Honey dishes with nub feet were produced in amber (1973-1977), amethyst (1989), etched amber (2001), aquamarine (1992-1996), etched aquamarine (1994), black (1983), chantilly green (1982), etched chantilly green (1983), coral (1989), crystal (1981-1982), etched crystal (1978-1981), decorated cranberry (1995), decorated ruby red (1995-1997), horizon blue (1982-1983), etched horizon blue (1982), ice blue (1983-1986), etched ice blue (1983), imperial blue (1988-1992), milk white (1978), peach (1993-1995), pink (1983), etched pink (1983-1988), plum (1999-2000), etched plum (2002), regal blue (1986), etched regal blue (1987), spruce green (1995-1998), and etched spruce green (2002).

Honey dishes with splayed feet were produced in amber, blue, crystal, milk white, sunset, and yellow. Most of these honey dishes were made in the 1950s, '60s, and '70s.

Color	Value
Amethyst	$16
Amethyst (etched)	$80
Amber	$45
Amber (splayed feet)	$215
Aquamarine	$40
Aquamarine (etched)	$115
Black	$55
Chantilly Green	$70
Chantilly Green (etched)	$74
Cranberry	$75
Crystal	$70
Crystal (splayed feet)	$290
Crystal (etched)	$65
Coral	$300
Decorated Ruby Red	$210
Horizon Blue	$30
Horizon Blue (splayed feet)	$450
Horizon Blue (etched)	$70
Ice Blue	$45
Ice Blue (etched)	$22
Imperial Blue	$75
Milk White	$100
Milk White (splayed feet)	$760
Peach	$40
Pink	$45
Pink (etched)	$65
Plum	$50
Plum (etched)	$80
Regal Blue	$55
Spruce Green	$20
Spruce Green (etched)	$50
Sunset (splayed feet)	$175
Yellow (splayed feet)	$660

Honey Dish, square honey dish w/ cover, spruce green, $20.00.

Honeycomb, #10

This pattern has become of particular interest to me. The pattern number indicates that it was an early issue, however, its appearance in catalogs and the like does not occur until the 1950s. I am still determining how many items exist for this pattern. I do know that it was manufactured in crystal in the 1950s, in amber and olive green in the 1960s, and in red-decorated in the early 1970s. In the early 1990s, Indiana took the sherbet, reworked the mold slightly, and created a new candle lamp. The candle lamp was made in an assortment of colors.

Honeycomb, oval handled relish, olive green, $8.00.

Item	Crystal	Amber	Olive Green	Red-Decorated
Bowl, pickle, oval, 2-handled	$5	$7	$8	$10
Bowl, relish, round, 2-handled, 7.5"	$8	$10	$11	$13
Plate, sherbet, 2-handled	$12	-	-	-
Sherbet	$8	-	-	-

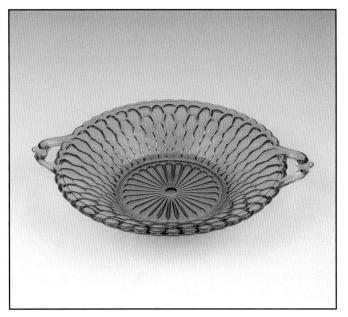

Honeycomb, round handled mint, amber, $10.00.

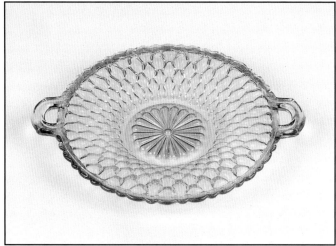

Honeycomb, round handled saucer, crystal with blue trim, $15.00.

Honeycomb, sherbet, crystal, $8.00.

Horseshoe

This tumbler was in constant production from 1905 to about 1930. You can find a variant of this tumbler with a star inside the horseshoe. Each tumbler is valued at $10.00.

Horseshoe, tumbler, crystal, $10.00.

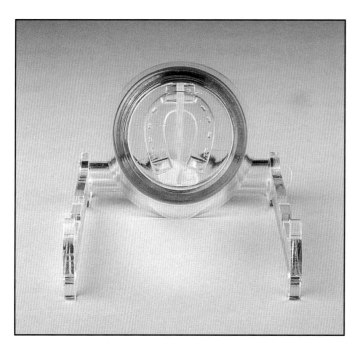

Horseshoe, tumbler, crystal, $10.00.

Kettle

Widely available from the mid-1960s and into the early 1970s, this item was mass-marketed through the florist trade as well as being sold in the department stores of the times. The *Kettle* was manufactured in matte black ($8) and milk white ($10). This item was also made in matte bronze and translucent red colors, although no value information could be gathered for these colors.

Kettle, black, $8.00.

Lace Edge

While Indiana issued a number of items with a lace edges, none were quite as generic as this candy box. Indiana created a candy/compote with a lace edge for both the *Lorain* pattern and the *Harvest* pattern. However, this item has a more simplistic ribbing pattern, allowing it to blend with many other patterns. One can find this item in a fired-on blue and a fired-on pink, which should place it being manufactured as early as the late 1950s. This item was also produced in amber ($16), crystal ($17), olive green ($15), iridescent blue ($42), horizon blue ($25), pink ($22), and teal ($50).

Lace Edge, candy box w/ cover, amber, $16.00.

Lord's Supper

The earliest version of this plate was made by Albany Glass. Indiana Glass acquired this mold in the early 1900s, made some minor changes, and had some limited production of the item, primarily in crystal and goofus glass. Indiana reissued the plate again for Tiara Exclusives in amber, aquamarine, burnt honey, crystal, peach, pink, sunset, and teal. There is not a whole lot of distinction in prices between the colors, with the exception of crystal and goofus. The value for the newer colored plates issued through Tiara is $20.00 - $25.00. The older crystal plates are valued at $50.00, while the newer crystal plates are valued at $10.00. Depending on how much paint is still on the goofus plate, their value can range from $15.00 to $25.00. These prices are for the larger 7" w x 11" l plate. Indiana also issued a "mini" lord's supper plate and a chalice (pictured here) which were also sold through Tiara Exclusives. These items are valued at $5.00 to $10.00.

Lord's Supper, chalice, crystal and crystal etched, $5.00.

Lord's Supper, plate, sunset, $25.00.

Nursery Rhymes

Several child's sets, were made by Indiana Glass over the years. The first was a set of four plates which had four nursery rhymes on them, including "Little Bo-Peep" (pattern #1), "Hey Diddle, Diddle" (pattern #2), "This Little Pig Went to Market" (pattern #3), and "The Three Bears" (pattern #4). Most of these items collectors will find in the marketplace are later editions of the originals. You can find them in a variety of colors including amber, light blue (pictured here), carnival blue, crystal, pink, and probably several other colors. To be an early issue (1905 - 1915) the plate must be either crystal or goofus decorated. If you own crystal, you can see if the plate fluoresces a yellow-green color under a black light. If it does not fluoresce, then it is a later production item. All colored items are later production items.

Another later made child's set (circa 1930) consisted of a plate, cup, bowl, tumbler, and pitcher. Again, this set was initially produced in crystal and green and was later manufactured and sold through Tiara Exclusives in many colors, including amber, light blue, cobalt blue, and pink. These items had lines from nursery rhymes, including "Humpty Dumpty" (pattern #246), and "See-Saw Margary Daw" (pattern #245), among others. The amber child's set was introduced in the late 1970s and was then produced in pink starting in the early 1980s. Indiana began producing this set in light blue by the mid-1980s. While the amber child's set was discontinued in the mid-1980s, the pink and blue sets were produced well into the late 1990s.

Item	Crystal	Amber	Pink	Blue
Bowl, cereal, 6.25" d	$21	$10	$12	$12
Mug, handled, 3.5" h	$25	$12	$12	$12
Pitcher, 5.25" h	$32	$15	$28	$28
Plate, Bo-Peep, 6.5" d	$30	$8	-	$12
Plate, Diddle, 6.5" d	$30	$8	-	$12
Plate, Little Pig, 6.5" d	$30	$8	-	$12
Plate, Bears, 6.5" d	$30	$8	-	$12
Plate, 3-part, 8.5" d	$22	$10	$15	$15
Tumbler, 4" h	$15	$10	$12	$12

Nursery Rhymes, plate & mug, amber, $10.00 & $12.00.

Nursery Rhymes, pair of children's plates, blue, $12.00.

Nursery Rhymes, pair of children's plates, blue, $12.00.

Petal

I was uncertain whether I wanted to include this pattern in this book. However, I see so much of this pattern in my travels I wanted to include it just to make collectors aware of its station in the glass collecting community. Federal Glass introduced this pattern in 1954 as their #2829 line and they manufactured it up until their closure in 1979. When Federal Glass closed its doors, Indiana acquired the molds and reproduced several of the bowls, starting in the early 1980s and continuing through the 1990s. While mainly produced in crystal, Indiana Glass also manufactured these bowls in light pink, light green, and light blue. The quality of the glass between Federal and Indiana is comparable and so mixing and matching should not be an issue. However, Indiana's version of these bowls appears to be made of slightly thicker glass, giving it a little more weight and the ability to stand up to a little more abuse. This pattern has many points (between ten and sixteen depending on the size of the item) and so it can easily be chipped. Remember all values are for mint condition items.

Petal, bowl, crystal, $15.00.

Item	Crystal	Green/ Blue/ Pink
Bowl, 6"	$13	-
Bowl, 8"	$13	-
Bowl, 10.5"	$15	$12
Plate, 9" d	$15	$12

Petal, pair of bowls, crystal & amber, saucer, crystal, $13.00 & $10.00.

Pineapple

Pineapple was initially issued in the early-1960s in milk white and then reissued through Tiara in the mid-1970s in horizon blue, lime green (pictured here), sunset (pictured here), light yellow, and ruby red. Teal was issued in the early 1990s and sold through Tiara Exclusives. Prices are consistent between the colors and range from $20 - $25.

Pineapple, pair of candleholders, green, $25.00.

Pineapple, pair of candleholders, sunset, $25.00.

Pioneer

This is another pattern I was unsure whether to include in this book. However, after seeing so much of it at flea markets, antique malls, yard sales, and the like, I decided to include it. This pattern was first manufactured by the Federal Glass Company during the 1940s. When Federal Glass closed its doors, Indiana acquired the molds and reproduced several of the serving items from the early 1980s through the 1990s. The quality of the glass between Federal and Indiana is comparable and so mixing and matching should not be an issue.

Item	Crystal
Bowl, w/fruit intaglio, 6.5" d	$10
Bowl, w/fruit intaglio, 11" d	$15
Plate, w/fruit intaglio, 12" d	$15

Pioneer, serving plate, crystal w/ intaglio, $15.00.

Pioneer, pair of bowls, crystal w/ intaglio, $20.00.

Princess

I am not quite sure how these items got lumped together, but they did. This very popular pattern is demanding some very nice prices, especially for the carnival glass items. The punch set can be found in crystal, iridescent blue, iridescent lime, and iridescent gold. The crystal punch set is very inexpensive due to the lack of demand. On the other hand, the carnival punch sets are in high demand, thereby making everyone dig a little deeper in the pocket if they want to take one home. These carnival punch sets sell like hotcakes during the holiday season because they make such a wonderful display. The candy boxes were made for many years and have always been a popular selling item. All the colors are widely available. Again, the iridescent colors will demand the higher prices with the iridescent lime leading the pack due to its scarcity. The amber ($14), crystal ($10), olive green ($14), ice blue ($14), light green ($12), and pink ($15) candy boxes are prevalent and make wonderful gifts. The production of these items began in the early 1970s and continued in production well in to the 1990s with the ice blue and pink colors being the last issues.

Princess, candy box w/ cover, amber, $14.00.

Item	Crystal	Blue	Green	Gold
Punch Bowl	$10	$80	$75	$60
Punch Cup	$2	$10	$7	$5
Punch Set	$20	$165	$145	$110

Princess, punch set, crystal, $20.00.

Royal

There are only a few items to include in this product line, a round candy box with a cover and a cigarette box with two individual ashtrays. The unique feature with this item is the faux bronze acorn finial on the cover, which adds an air of distinction to the product. This pattern was produced after the merger with Lancaster Colony and therefore does not have a pattern number. Manufactured throughout the 1960s, one can find these items in amber, crystal, milk white, and olive green. The candy box for this pattern resurfaced again in the mid-1980s when it was marketed through Tiara Exclusives. However, this time it was manufactured in black and did not have the acorn finial. Instead, it was sold with a polished silver-colored finial.

Item	Crystal	Olive Green	Amber	Black
Candy Box w/cover	$10	$15	$15	$25
Cigarette Box w/cover	$5	$10	$10	-

Royal, candy box w/ cover, amber, $15.00.

Strawberry, #32

I do not think there are any other items associated with this pattern number, but I wish there were. This compote was known to be manufactured as early as the 1950s, but in all probability was produced even earlier. Initially it was produced only in crystal, but was later reissued through Tiara Exclusives in a variety of colors, including sunset (pictured here) and imperial blue ($20).

Strawberry, compote w/ cover, sunset, $25.00.

Top Hat

Widely available from the mid-1960s and into the early 1970s, this item was mass-marketed through the florist trade as well as being sold in the department stores of the times. The top hat was manufactured in crystal ($12), matte black, matte blue, matte pink, milk white ($10), olive green ($12), translucent amber, translucent blue, and translucent red. The crystal top hat was brought back in the mid-1980s, only this time it was filled with wax and sold as a candle. This was yet another example of Indiana's creativity and continual practice of adapting already existing products into new sales ideas. A number of companies produced this style top hat, including Fenton.

Top Hat, crystal & olive green, $12.00 & $12.00.

Catalogs

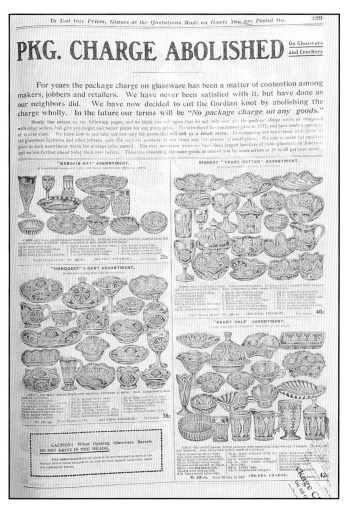

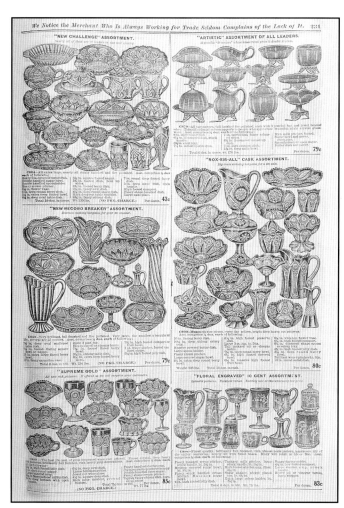

Butler Brothers Catalog #580, Mid-Summer 1906, page 229, upper right corner - mixed "Twin Feathers", "Shooting Star", & "Double Pinwheel" assortment.

Butler Brothers Catalog #580, Mid-Summer 1906, page 231, middle right - mixed "Nogi", "Twin Feathers", & "Double Pinwheel" assortment.

Butler Brothers Catalog #878, Mid-Spring 1911, page 114, lower right corner - "Pattern #125" & "Pattern #253" assortment.

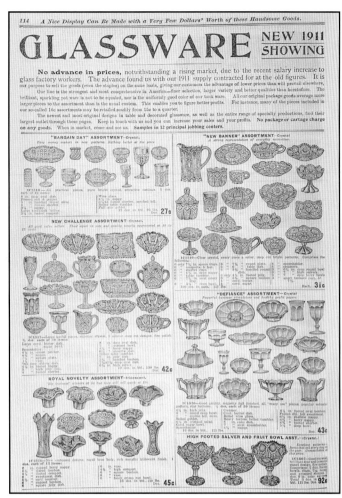

Butler Brothers Catalog #1061, Mid-Winter 1913, page 121, upper right corner - "Paneled Heather" assortment.

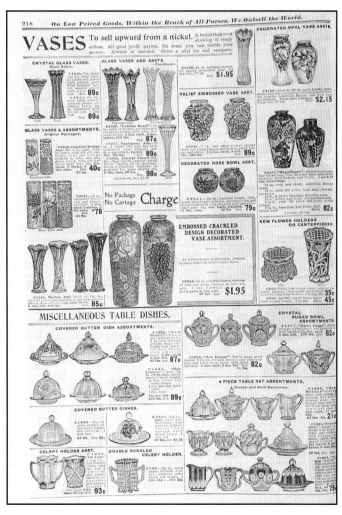

Butler Brothers Catalog #1119, Mid-Summer 1913, page 218, lower left corner - "Bosc Pear", Bethlehem Star", & "Rose Point Band" butters, lower right corner - "Bethlehem Star" & Bosc Pear" sugars, "Bethlehem Star" butter, "Bosc Pear" sugar, "Bosc Pear" spooner, & "Bethlehem Star" creamer.

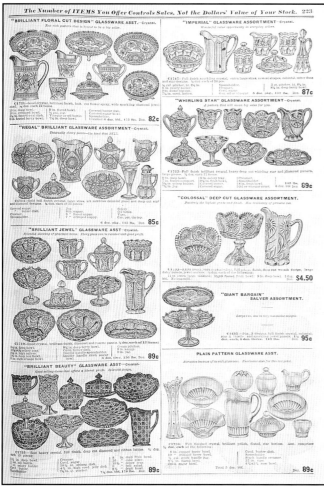

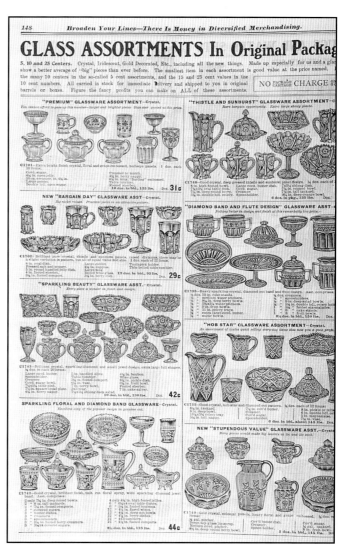

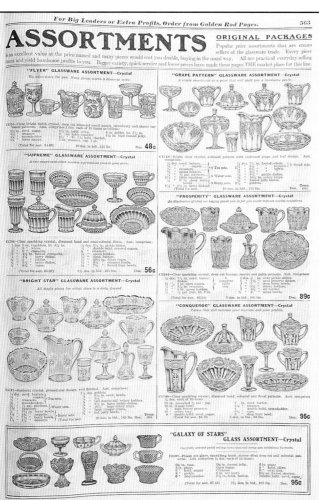

Butler Brothers Catalog #1119, Mid-Summer 1913, page 223, upper left corner - "Rose Point Band" assortment.

Butler Brothers Catalog #1228, July 1914, page 148, lower left corner - "Rose Point Band" assortment.

Butler Brothers Catalog #1502, June 1917, page 563, upper right corner - "Late Paneled Grape" assortment, left center - "Starband" assortment, "Bethlehem Star" assortment.

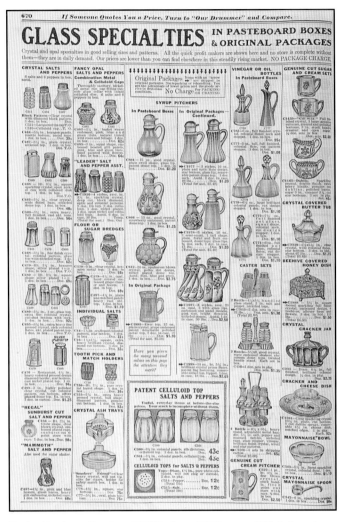

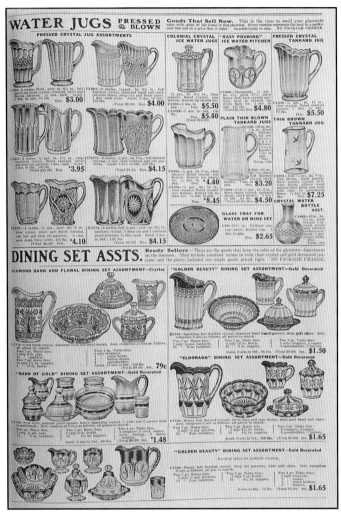

Butler Brothers Catalog #1502, June 1917, page 570, left center - honey dish w/ beehive pattern.

Butler Brothers Catalog #1752, Spring 1920, top center - "Starband" & "Flower Medallion" pitchers, left center "Horsemint" assortment, right center - "Starband" assortment.

Butler Brothers Catalog #1752, Spring 1920, top left corner - "Flower Medallion" & "Starband" sugars, top center - "Starband" & "Flower Medallion" celery vases, left center - "Starband", "Bethlehem Star", & "Flower Medallion" creamers, left top corner - "Bethlehem Star" & "Pattern #75" compotes, right center - "Honey Dish" w/ beehive pattern & "Rayed Flower" honey dish, center row - "Horsemint" butter, "Bethlehem Star" creamer, & "Late Paneled Grape" spooner and sugar, lower left corner - "Bethlehem Star" & "Pattern #163" berry/salad sets.

Butler Brothers Catalog #1888, Mid-Summer 1921, page 155, middle right - "Success" & "Bethlehem Star" blank sugars, "Horsemint" butter, "Bethlehem Star" creamer, "Late Paneled Grape" spooner and sugar, center - "Starband" & "Flower Medallion" celery vases, "Success" & "Bethlehem Star" blank creamers, bottom - "Bethlehem Star" blank, "Narcissus Spray", & "Pattern #125" creamers, butters, and sugars.

Clockwise from top left:
Butler Brothers Catalog
#1888, Mid-Summer 1921,
page 165, left center -
"Starband" assortment,
"Narcissus Spray" assort-
ment, left bottom corner -
mixed "Pattern #125" &
"Pattern #253"

Butler Brothers Catalog
#1888, Mid-Summer 1921,
page 166, top left corner -
"Horsemint" assortment,
"Starband" assortment,
bottom left corner -
"Narcissus Spray" goofus
painted plate and bowl,
second row from bottom -
"Pattern #164" &
"Starband" fluted bowls.

Butler Brothers Catalog
#2102, September 1923,
page 407, upper right
corner - "Late Paneled
Grape" sugar and spooner,
"Horsemint" creamer and
butter, middle center -
"Starband", "Bethlehem
Star", & "Flower Medal-
lion" creamers, butters, and
sugars, middle right -
"Starband" and "Flower
Medallion" celery vases.

Butler Brothers Catalog
#2447, April 1927, page
153, second row from top -
"Gothic Windows" &
"Pattern #164" creamers,
sugars, and butters, left
center - "Pattern #164"
sugar and tumbler,
"Bethlehem Star" creamer,
"Gothic Windows" butter,
"Pattern #163" &
"Starband" celery vases,
lower right corner -
"Bethlehem Star" berry/
salad bowls.

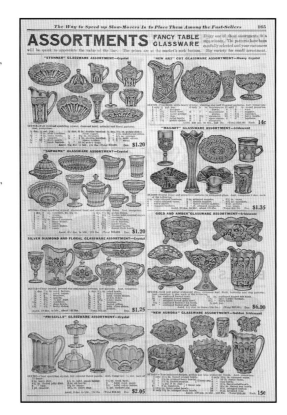

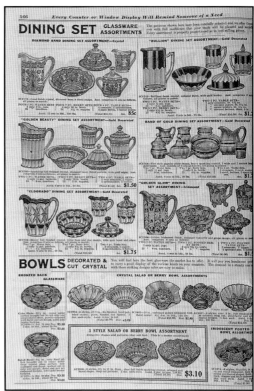

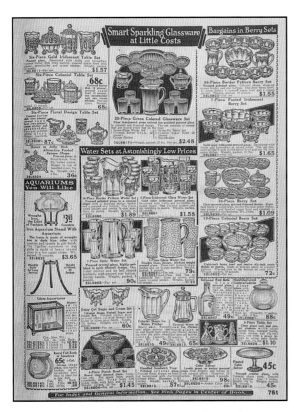

Sears, Roebuck & Co. Catalog #156, Spring/Summer 1928, page 751, upper right corner "Gothic Windows" berry/salad set, upper left corner "Gothic Windows" water set, upper left corner "Narcissus Spray" breakfast set, upper left corner "Flower Medallion" honey dish, bottom center, "Early American" handled serving tray.

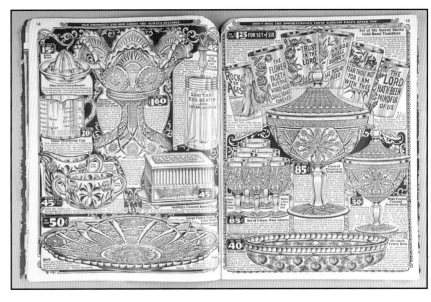

Top right:
Lee's Catalog, 1928, center left page "Lords Supper" plate.

Center right:
Lee's Catalog, 1928, "Rosette with Pinwheels".

Bottom right:
Lee's Catalog, 1928, "Rosette with Pinwheels".

Butler Brothers Catalog #4545, Spring 1938, page 123, upper right corner - painted mixed set of "Double Fleur de Lis", "Pattern #602", "Pattern #603", & "Pattern #257."

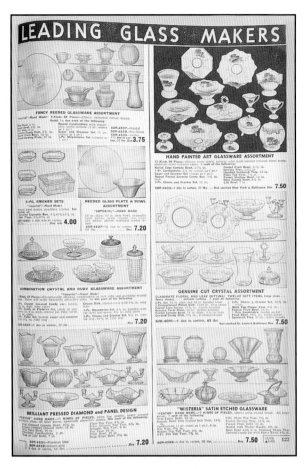

Butler Brothers Catalog #4851, Holiday 1942-1943, page 478, top center - "Willow" assortment, bottom center - "Paneled Daisies and Finecut" punch set.

Butler Brothers Catalog #4851, Holiday 1942-1943, page 479, top row - "Mirrorglas" assortment, formally known as "Pattern #1005", second row - "Constellation" assortment, third row - "Garland" assortment,

Indiana Glass Catalog, 1967, "Diamond Point."

Top right:
Indiana Glass Catalog, 1967, left side "Monticello", right side "Midas."

Center right:
Indiana Glass Catalog, 1967, left top "Wild Cherry", left bottom "Mint", right side "Olive."

Bottom right:
Indiana Glass Catalog, 1967, left side "Gold and Platinum", right side "Pewtertone."

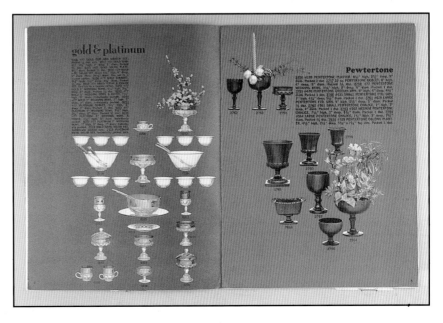

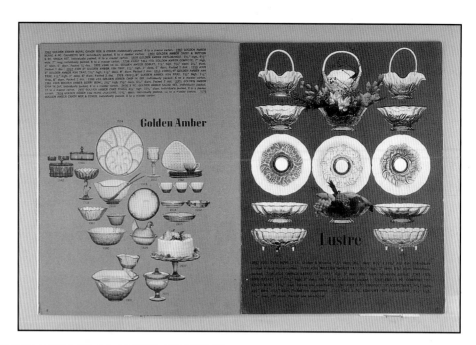

Indiana Glass Catalog,
1967, right side "Golden
Amber", left side "Lustre."

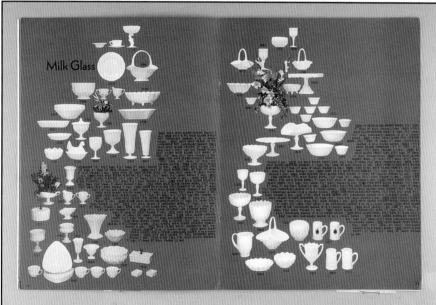

Indiana Glass Catalog,
1967, "Milk Glass."

Indiana Glass Catalog,
1967, "Crystal."

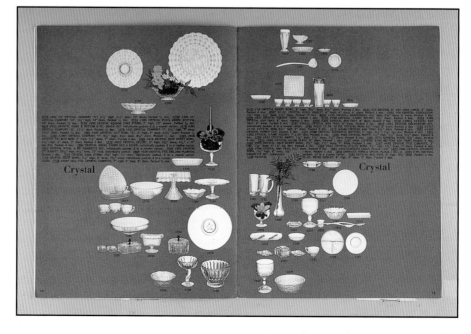

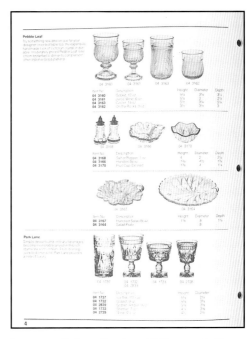

S & H Green Stamps Catalog, 1971, left page "Harvest" in milk white, right page "Whitehall" and "King's Crown" in olive green.

Lancaster Colony Catalog, 1980, rows 1, 2, and 3 - "Pebble Leaf" assortment, bottom row - "Park Lane" assortment.

The History Of Glass

Over 4,000 years ago, perhaps on the Sands of Egypt, Syria, or Babylonia, the manufacturing of glass began. Since then mankind has added, little by little, to the glassmaker's art. The skill of the glassmaker has been a source of beauty treasured by all people.

Making glassware by hand is the oldest industry in America. It started in the Jamestown Colony in 1608.

In the manufacture of Tiara Exclusives many of the techniques and tools of the early days are used. It is natural that you, a Tiara Customer, should want to know something about the way the line is created. Much of it is hand made, either pressed or blown, and in molds dating back many, many years. Each item is exclusive with Tiara, and will not be found in any other line.

Glass is made of silica, soda ash, lime, and feldspar. Small amounts of various other chemicals such as copper, selenium, manganese, cadmium, etc. are added to make a "batch." After careful mixing of the selected ingredients, a quantity of broken glass — called cullet — is often added to the "batch" mixture to speed up the melting process. Glass is truly the product of earth and fire! The tank into which the glassworker shovels the "batch" has been pre-fired to an intense heat of about 2700°F. In about 18 hours the glass is ready to be gathered and blown. It takes a shop of six to 18 skilled workers to make one item.

A blowpipe is a hollow tube of steel with a special "head" which the gatherer slips into the tank of molten glass. Turning it in the glass, he gathers just the right "gob" on the end of the pipe. He hands it to the blower after first shaping on a marveling plate. The blower then shapes the "ball" with apple-wood tools and paddles, and with carefully controlled puffs, forms a hollow bulb. His tools are varied and adapted for each item, and include the Pucellas, often called just the "tool." Like a huge pair of tweezers, the "tool" becomes a set of additional fingers for the skilled craftsman.

Now the piece is ready to be removed from the blowpipe and turned over to the stick-up boy, who picks it up and takes it to the "glory-hole," a reheating furnace kept at about 2500°F. Here the glass is reheated and taken to the finisher for shaping. He, with the skilled touch of practiced hands, forms the decanter, bowl, pitcher, etc. When the item is to have a handle, or requires additional work, it is handed to a second finisher.

As this finisher completes the piece, a carry-in boy appears with a special fork, snaps the piece from the punty and carries it to an annealing oven or "lehr." Here it travels on a slowly moving, endless chain through several hours of diminishing heat, emerging at the end ready to be inspected. It is then labeled with a Tiara Exclusive's sticker, boxed and put in stock.

Since many Tiara items are blown and shaped by hand, variations in size, shape and color lend real individuality to each item.

Tiara Exclusives Catalog, 1981, "The History of Glass" according to Indiana Glass.

Tiara Exclusives Catalog, 1981, "Sandwich" or "Early American" in amber.

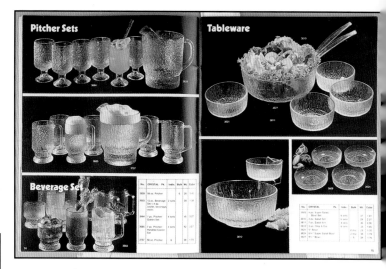

Indiana Glass Catalog, 1982, "Crystal Ice" assortment.

Indiana Glass Catalog, 1982, "Whitehall" assortment.

Indiana Glass Catalog, 1982, candy box assortment including "Mt. Vernon", "Princess", "Beaded Edge", Hen on a Nest", "King's Crown", "Lace Edge", and "Lily Pons."

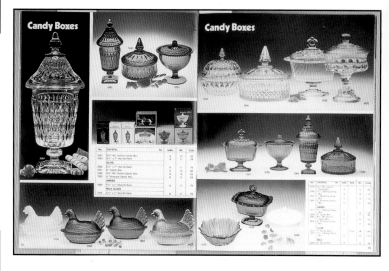

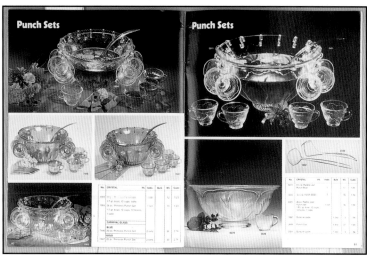

Indiana Glass Catalog, 1982, punch set assortment including "Princess" and "Pebble Leaf."

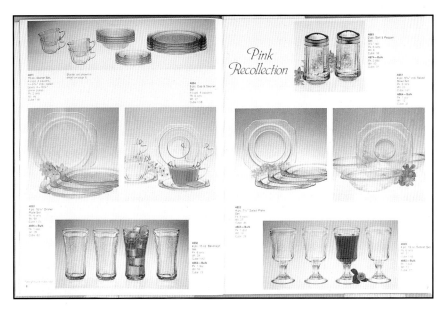

Indiana Glass Catalog, 1984, "Recollection" assortment in pink.

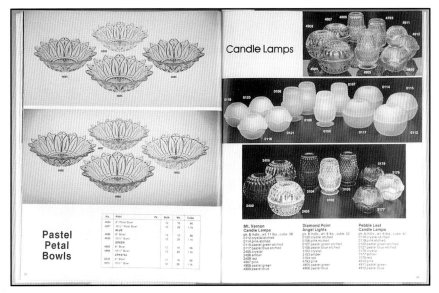

Indiana Glass Catalog, 1984, left side – "Petal" assortment in crystal and various pastel colors, right side – candle lamp assortment including "Diamond Point", "Mt. Vernon", and "Pebble Leaf."

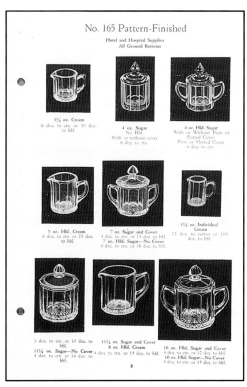

Indiana Glass Catalog, c.1940, "Pattern #165" assortment.

Indiana Glass Catalog, c.1940, "Pattern #253" assortment.

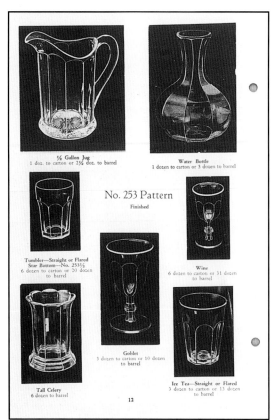

No. 253 Pattern
Finished

½ Gallon Jug
1 doz. to carton or 2½ doz. to barrel

Water Bottle
1 dozen to carton or 3 to barrel

Tumbler—Straight or Flared
Star Bottom—No. 253½
6 dozen to carton or 20 dozen
to barrel

Wine
6 dozen to carton or 31 dozen
to barrel

Goblet
3 dozen to carton or 10 dozen
to barrel

Tall Celery
6 dozen to barrel

Ice Tea—Straight or Flared
3 dozen to carton or 13 dozen
to barrel

12

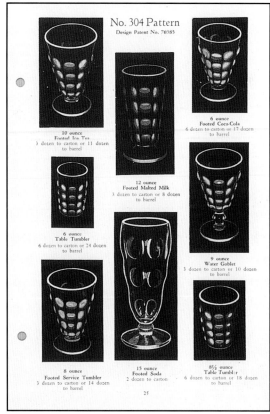

No. 304 Pattern
Design Patent No. 76985

10 ounce
Footed Ice Tea
3 dozen to carton or 11 dozen
to barrel

6 ounce
Footed Coca-Cola
6 dozen to carton or 17 dozen
to barrel

12 ounce
Footed Malted Milk
3 dozen to carton or 8 dozen
to barrel

6 ounce
Table Tumbler
6 dozen to carton or 24 dozen
to barrel

9 ounce
Water Goblet
3 dozen to carton or 10 dozen
to barrel

8 ounce
Footed Service Tumbler
3 dozen to carton or 14 dozen
to barrel

15 ounce
Footed Soda
2 dozen to carton

8½ ounce
Table Tumbler
6 dozen to carton or 18 dozen
to barrel

25

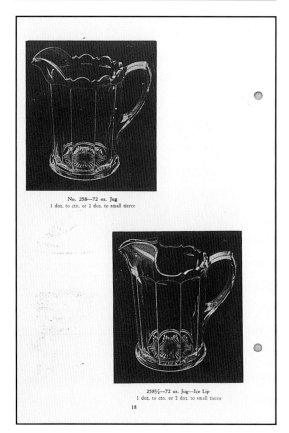

No. 258—72 oz. Jug
1 doz. to ctn. or 2 doz. to small tierce

258½—72 oz. Jug—Ice Lip
1 doz. to ctn. or 2 doz. to small tierce

18

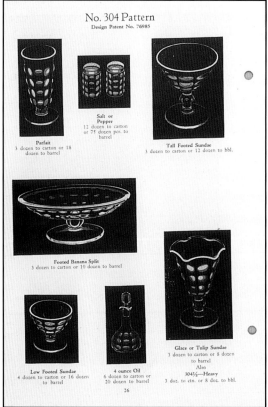

No. 304 Pattern
Design Patent No. 76985

Parfait
3 dozen to carton or 18
dozen to barrel

Salt or
Pepper
12 dozen to carton
or 75 dozen pcs. to
barrel

Tall Footed Sundae
3 dozen to carton or 12 dozen to bbl.

Footed Banana Split
3 dozen to carton or 10 dozen to barrel

Low Footed Sundae
4 dozen to carton or 16 dozen
to barrel

4 ounce Oil
6 dozen to carton or
20 dozen to barrel

Glace or Tulip Sundae
3 dozen to carton or 8 dozen
to barrel
Also
304½—Heavy
3 doz. to ctn. or 8 doz. to bbl.

26

Top left:
Indiana Glass Catalog, c.1940, "Pattern #253" assortment.

Bottom left:
Indiana Glass Catalog, c.1940, "Pattern #258" pitchers.

Top right:
Indiana Glass Catalog, c.1940, "Pattern #304" assortment.

Bottom right:
ndiana Glass Catalog, c.1940, "Pattern #304" assortment.

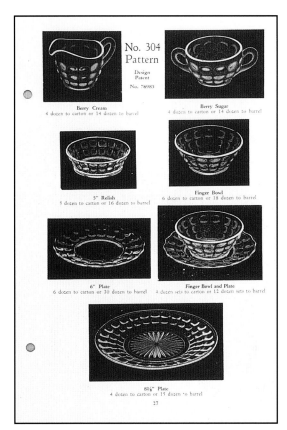

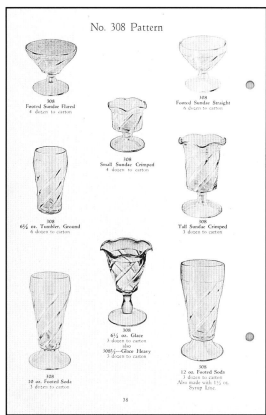

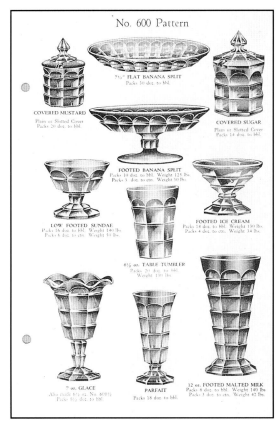

Top left:
Indiana Glass Catalog, c.1940, "Pattern #304" assortment.

Bottom left:
Indiana Glass Catalog, c.1940, "Pattern #600" assortment.

Top right:
Indiana Glass Catalog, c.1940, "Pattern #308" assortment.

*Bottom right:*ndiana Glass Catalog, c.1940, "Pattern #308"
assortment, "Pattern #253" punch bowl.

Indiana Glass Catalog, c.1940, "Pattern #350" assortment.

Indiana Glass Catalog, c.1940, "Pattern #350" assortment.

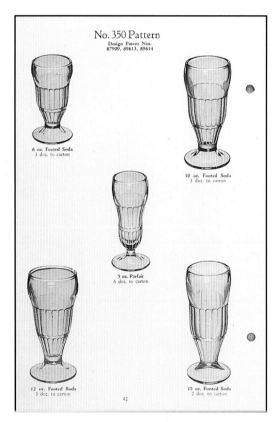

Indiana Glass Catalog, c.1940, "Pattern #350" assortment.

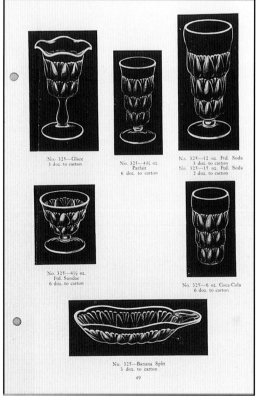

Indiana Glass Catalog, c.1940, "Pattern #325" assortment.

References

Books

Adler, Donna. *Indiana Glass Company of Dunkirk, Indiana. 1907-2002.*

Bond, Marcella. *The Beauty of Albany Glass 1893-1902.* Berne, Indiana: Publishers Printing House, 1972.

Breadahoft, Tom & Neil. *Fifty Years of Collectible Glass 1920-1970: Easy Identification and Price Guide, Vol. II.* Iola, WI: Krause Publications, 2000.

Edwards, Bill & Mike Carwile. *Standard Encyclopedia of Pressed Glass 1860-1930.* Paducah, Kentucky: Collector Books, 1999.

Felt, Tom & Elaine and Rich Stoer. *The Glass Candlestick Book, Volume 2.* Paducah, Kentucky: Collector Books, 2003.

Florence, Gene. *Collectible Glassware from the 40s, 50s and 60s, An Illustrated Value Guide.* 6th Edition. Paducah, Kentucky: Collector Books, 2000.

Florence, Gene. *Collectors Encyclopedia of Depression Glass, 15th Edition.* Paducah, Kentucky: Collector Books, 2002.

Florence, Gene. *Florence's Glassware Pattern Identification Guide, Volume II.* Paducah, Kentucky: Collector Books, 2000.

Husfloen, Kentuckyle. *American Pressed Glass and Bottles: Price Guide.* Dubuque, Iowa: Antique Trader Books, 1994.

Husfloen, Kentuckyle. *Collector's Guide to American Pressed Glass 1825-1915.* Iola, Wisconsin: Krause Publications, 1992.

Jenks, Bill & Jerry Luna. *Early American Pattern Glass 1850-1910: Major Collectible Table Settings with Prices.* Radnor, Pennsylvania: Wallace Homestead Book Company. 1990.

Jenks, Bill & Darryl Reilly. *Early American Pattern Glass: Collector's Identification & Price Guide.* 2nd Edition. Iola, Wisconsin. Krause Publications, 2002.

Kamm, Minnie Watson. *Two Hundred Pattern Glass Pitchers.* Detroit, Michigan: Motschall Company, 1939.

Kamm, Minnie Watson. *A Second Two Hundred Pattern Glass Pitchers.* Detroit, Michigan: Motschall Company, 1940.

Kamm, Minnie Watson. *A Third Two Hundred Pattern Glass Pitchers.* Detroit, Michigan: Graphic Arts Process Corp., 1943.

Kamm, Minnie Watson. *A Fourth Pitcher Book, 2nd Edition.* Grosse Point Farm, Michigan:1950.

Kamm, Minnie Watson. *A Fifth Pitcher Book.* Grosse Point Farm, Michigan:1948.

Kamm, Minnie Watson. *A Sixth Pitcher Book.* Grosse Point, Farm, Michigan:1949.

Kamm, Minnie Watson. *A Seventh Pitcher Book.* Grosse Point, Michigan:1953.

Kamm, Minnie Watson. *An Eighth Pitcher Book.* Detroit, Michigan: Kamm Publications, 1954.

Kovel, Ralph & Terry. *Kovels Antiques and Collectibles Price List 2000, 32nd Edition.* New York, New York: Three Rivers Press, 2000.

Kovel, Ralph & Terry. *Kovels Depression Glass and Dinnerware, 7th Edition.* New York, New York: Three Rivers Press, 2001.

McCain, Mollie Helen. *The Collector's Encyclopedia of Pattern Glass, 2nd Edition.* Paducah, Kentucky: Collector Books, 1992.

McKearin, George S. & Helen. New York: Crown Publishers, 1941.

Schroy, Ellen T. *Warman's Depression Glass: A Value and Identification Guide, 2nd Edition.* Iola Wisconsin: Krause Publications, 2000.

Story, William. *Indiana Pressed Glass From The Gas-Boom Era.* Muncie, Indiana: Ball State University, 1977.

Stout, Sandra McPhee. *Depression Glass: Number One in Color, 3rd Edition.* Des Moines, Iowa: Wallace Homestead Book Company, 1970.

Teal, Ron, Sr. *Tiara Exclusives: Company Catalog Reprints.* Marietta, Ohio: Antique Publications, 2000.

Weatherman, Hazel Marie. *Colored Glassware of the Depression Era, 2nd Edition.* Springfield, MO: Hazel Marie Weatherman. 1970.

Weatherman, Hazel Marie. *Colored Glassware of the Depression Era 2, 2nd Edition.* Springfield, MO: Weatherman Glass Books. 1974.

Trade Catalogs

Butler Brothers China & Glassware 1925. Signal Mountain, Tennessee: Antiques Research Publications, 1968.

Butler Brothers China & Glassware 1930. Mentone, Alabama: Antiques Research Publications, 1968.

Butler Brothers Glassware 1905. Chattanooga, Tennessee: Antiques Research Publications.

Butler Brothers Glassware 1910. Chattanooga, Tennessee: Antiques Research Publications.

Hotel-Restaurant and Soda Fountain Glassware. Indiana Glass Company, Dunkirk, Indiana: Indiana Glass Company, 1957.

Indiana Glass Company Catalog. Dunkirk, Indiana. Indiana Glass Company, 193?.

Indiana Glass Company Catalog. Dunkirk, Indiana. Indiana Glass Company, 1932.

Indiana Glass Company Catalog. Dunkirk, Indiana. Indiana Glass Company, 1969.

Indiana Glass Company Catalog. Dunkirk, Indiana. Indiana Glass Company, 1975.

Lancaster Colony Commercial Products: Indiana Glass Catalog. Columbus, Ohio: Lancaster Colony, 1980.

Lancaster Colony Commercial Products: Indiana Glass Catalog. Columbus, Ohio: Lancaster Colony, 1984.

Our Drummer #194: Butler Brothers Company. New York, NY, Spring & Summer 1898.

Our Drummer #428: Butler Brothers Company. New York, NY, July 1902.

Our Drummer #456: Butler Brothers Company. St. Louis, MO, Spring 1903.

Our Drummer #580: Butler Brothers Company. Chicago, IL, Mid-Summer 1906.

Our Drummer #596: Butler Brothers Company. New York, NY, Mid-Winter 1907.

Our Drummer #856: Butler Brothers Company. Chicago, IL, February 1911.

Our Drummer #878: Butler Brothers Company. New York, NY, Mid-Spring 1911.

Our Drummer #1061: Butler Brothers Company. New York, NY, Mid-Winter 1913.

Our Drummer #1119: Butler Brothers Company. Chicago, IL, Mid-Summer 1913.

Our Drummer #1142: Butler Brothers Company. New York, NY, Fall 1913.

Our Drummer #1228: Butler Brothers Company. New York, NY, July 1915.

Our Drummer #1502: Butler Brothers Company. Chicago, IL, June 1917.

Our Drummer #1752: Butler Brothers Company. New York, NY, Spring 1920.

Our Drummer #1888: Butler Brothers Company. Chicago, IL, Mid-Summer 1921.

Our Drummer #2102: Butler Brothers Company. New York, NY, September 1923.

Our Drummer #2447: Butler Brothers Company. New York, NY, April 1927.

Our Drummer #2716: Butler Brothers Company. Minneapolis, MN, May 1930.

Our Drummer #2897: Butler Brothers Company. Baltimore, MD, July 1932.

Our Drummer #2939: Butler Brothers Company. Baltimore, MD, October 1932.

Our Drummer #4112: Butler Brothers Company. Baltimore, MD, Summer 1934.

Our Drummer #4259: Butler Brothers Company. Baltimore, MD, July-August 1935.

Our Drummer #4360: Butler Brothers Company. San Francisco, CA, May-June 1936.

Our Drummer #4445: Butler Brothers Company. New York, NY, Spring 1937.

Our Drummer #4519: Butler Brothers Company. San Francisco, CA, Fall & Holiday 1938.

Our Drummer #4545: Butler Brothers Company. St. Louis, MO, Spring 1938.

Our Drummer #4689: Butler Brothers Company. San Francisco, CA, Summer 1939.

Our Drummer #4762: Butler Brothers Company. St. Louis, MO, Fall 1940.

Our Drummer #4829: Butler Brothers Company. San Francisco, CA, Spring 1940.

Our Drummer #4851: Butler Brothers Company. Chicago, IL, Fall & Winter 1942.

Our Drummer #4858: Butler Brothers Company. Chicago, IL, Spring 1942.

Price List No.52: Indiana Glassware. Dunkirk, Indiana: Indiana Glass Company, 1952.

Price List No.63: Indiana Glassware. Dunkirk, Indiana: Indiana Glass Company, 1962.

Syndicated and Independent Variety Stores Glassware: Indiana Glass Company. Dunkirk, Indiana: Indiana Glass Company, 1956.

The Catalogue: Indiana Glass Company. Dunkirk, Indiana: Indiana Glass Company, 1982.

The Catalogue: Indiana Glass Company. Dunkirk, Indiana: Indiana Glass Company, 1985.

The Catalogue: Indiana Glass Company. Dunkirk, Indiana: Indiana Glass Company, 1986.

The Catalogue: Indiana Glass Company. Dunkirk, Indiana: Indiana Glass Company, 1988-1989.

Tiara Exclusives Catalogs. Dunkirk, Indiana: Indiana Glass Company, 1981 - 1998.

Variety Store Catalog. Indiana Glass Company, Dunkirk, Indiana: Indiana Glass Company, 1956.

Magazine Articles

"Depression Glass." *Old Madrid or New Recollection. Antiques & Collectors Reproduction News*. November 1996. pp. 121-124.

"Glass Review." *Depression Glass*. November 1979. pp. 44-47

Koch, Nora. "Indiana Glass Makes Recollection in Crystal." *Depression Glass Daze*.

Iwen, Marg. "Indiana Glass." *Glass Collector's Digest*. December/January 1995. pp. 42-54.

Sionakides, Roni. "Indiana Catalog Circa 1932." *Depression Glass Daze*. March 1980. pp. 29-34.

"Some Childrens Plates Never Grow Old." *Antiques & Collectors Reproduction News*. July 2001. pp. 80-81

Websites

Adler, Donna. "History of Indiana Glass." http://www.indianaglass.carnivalheaven.com/. 2003.

Hartwell, Ken. "Tiara Exclusives History 1970-1998." http://www.geocities.com/tiaraman1947/.

Krupey, Joyce E. "Patterns Important to the History of Depression Glass. National Depression Glass Association." http://www.ndga.net/. 2003.

Specialty Internet Auctions. http://www.justglass.com/. 2003.

Stutzman, Ray. "Pattern Glass Enthusiast & Collector, Early American Pattern Glass." http://www.home1.gte.net/thunerb/.

Walls, Leonette A. "Indiana Glass Company's Willow (aka) 'Oleander'." http://www.justglass-online.com/. 2003.

Whitehorn, David. "Double Pinwheel. Early American Pattern Glass Society." http://www.eapgs.org/doublepinwheel/.

Notes